Francis Hueffer

Richard Wagner and the Music of the Future

History and aesthetics

Francis Hueffer

Richard Wagner and the Music of the Future
History and aesthetics

ISBN/EAN: 9783337385903

Printed in Europe, USA, Canada, Australia, Japan

Cover: Foto ©ninafisch / pixelio.de

More available books at **www.hansebooks.com**

RICHARD WAGNER

AND THE

MUSIC OF THE FUTURE.

HISTORY AND ÆSTHETICS.

BY

FRANZ HUEFFER.

LONDON:
CHAPMAN AND HALL, 193, PICCADILLY.
1874.

The Right of Translation is Reserved.

PRINTED BY TAYLOR AND CO.,
LITTLE QUEEN STREET, LINCOLN'S INN FIELDS.

PREFACE.

A CONSIDERABLE part of the contents of the present volume has been previously published in the 'Fortnightly Review;' a smaller portion, consisting chiefly of the letters of R. Schumann, appeared in the 'Academy.' Everything, however, has been recast and made subservient to the purposes of this book, about which the author now begs leave to make a few introductory remarks.

Musicians and theorists of all colours (for now-a-days one must distinguish the different shades of party opinion, in music as well as in politics or religion) agree in the one point, that, by the works of Beethoven's latter years, and especially by the Ninth Symphony of that master, a new phase is marked in the history of their art. In the last-mentioned work, or, to speak quite accurately, in its three first movements, it was finally shown, how far music in its separate condition could go in achieving the ultimate aim of all art, *i.e.*, the rendering of the emotions of the human heart. It may in this respect be called the triumph of absolute music; and, indeed, no symphonic work of a later period can be said to have surpassed, or even equalled in beauty and power of expression, this gigantic effort of a master-mind. But in this very splendour of artistic perfection we indistinctly, but no less certainly, feel the want of something that remains unexpressed; and by acknowledging this want, as founded in the nature of music itself, and introducing into the last movement of his D minor symphony the human word, as a firm basis for his lofty aspirations, Beethoven has at the same time ushered in a new period of his art.

To define the æsthetical foundation of this new idea in music, and at the same time follow the course of its growth, will be my chief task in the following pages. Here I will only try to indicate in a few words its most general characteristics, and first of all to fix its nondescript airiness into a local habitation and a name. The new movement, therefore, which arose after and, to a great extent, through Beethoven's reformatory deeds, we will henceforth call the period of *poetic music* (the strict definition of which term I must defer to another occasion); or, in case the reader should prefer an old to a new-coined expression, we will occasionally apply the generally acknowledged *sobriquet* of the Music of the Future.

The poetic principle, alluded to, may be divided into a lyrical and a dramatic part; which distinction, translated into musical terms, will lead us to the two important forms of the *Music-Drama* and the *Song*. At the same time it seems to me that only in these two kinds of development music shows a decided advance upon Beethoven's creations, a remark which, of course, is made without any derogatory tendency with regard to the instrumental works of modern composers. In many cases these have displayed individual beauties of the highest order without, however, adding essentially new features to the symphonic form, as established by Beethoven.

As a further means of subdivision, I have headed the single chapters of my work with the representative names of Richard Wagner for the dramatic, and Franz Schubert, Robert Schumann, Franz Liszt, and Robert Franz for the different shades of the lyrical phase of modern music.

I.

The Drama.

"Blest pair of Sirens, pledges of heaven's joy,
 Sphere-born harmonious sisters, Voice and Verse,
 Wed your divine sounds, and mix'd power employ,
 Dead things with inbreath'd sense able to pierce."
                                             Milton.

CHAPTER 1.

RICHARD WAGNER.

1.

If I were asked for a striking point of distinction between musicians of the old and modern schools, I should mention, first of all, their essentially altered position with regard to literature in general. During the last century, a musician was expected to study, from his very childhood, all the intricacies, both theoretical and practical, of his art, but beyond this his education, as a rule, showed the most deplorable deficiencies; and whenever he had to write on ordinary foolscap, instead of the accustomed staff of five lines, his hand seemed to shake and his thought to stammer. Mozart, for instance, seems to have been decidedly not above the average level of middle-class education at his time; and to connect the idea of a thinker with good old "papa Haydn," who, while composing his *Creation*, used to mumble a couple of 'Ave Maria's' when the source of his inspiration ceased to flow, seems grotesquely incongruous. Indeed, with the sole exception of Gluck, no first-rate musician of the eighteenth century can be named who would not have shrunk from the idea of giving literary evidence as to the fundamental principles of his own art; a phenomenon which, in most cases, finds its explanation in the mentioned circumstance of an exclusively technical education. Beethoven's youth also was passed in a purely professional atmosphere; but his powerful mind soon expanded with interests of a wider range. Plutarch was his favourite author, and verses of Homer were frequently found, interspersed with those puzzling economical calculations and musical sketches which covered the walls of his room and the scraps of paper on his writing-table. His æsthetical thoughts also display the intuitive depth of his great nature. Still the language of illiterate awkwardness in which they were clad, as far, at least, as we may judge from Schindler's account, distinctly shows a want of early training.

We receive a very different impression as we turn to the literary capabilities of representative modern composers. It is true that Mendelssohn refrained, on principle, from untraditional theoretic utterances, although the fluent grace of his style shows to great advantage in his private letters. But Schumann went through a regular course of university studies, and after that was the editor of a musical journal for many years, before his name as a composer became known beyond the circle of his immediate admirers. The literary style of Liszt too reflects clearly the suppleness and grace of his refined genius, although, in his case, one might suppose that the unequalled mastery of his instrument, which he displayed as *enfant prodige* from his earliest youth, would have engrossed the attention even of the most precocious intellect.

These few remarks seemed required to assist the reader in seeing in its true light one of the numerous accusations which Wagner's innumerable enemies have raised against his creative power. It is grounded on the fact of his having investigated the metaphysical and historical sides of his art.

The two faculties of speculation and execution—these wise men assert—are never found combined in the same individuality, and on the strength of this axiom, they prove *a priori* that the author of *Oper und Drama* cannot but produce works of cold deliberation, which, based on theoretical speculation, may occasionally attain effects of skill, but must needs lack the life of spontaneous production. To refute the arguments of such theorists by the intrinsic value of Wagner's creations would be in vain, as these appeal altogether to a higher kind of receptive faculty, than is to be found amongst the high-priests of orthodox Philistinism. Such men never will or can conceive that, in art, as well as in life, we must distinguish between the state of Paradisiac innocence and that of self-conscious knowledge. In the former the feelings are poured forth with almost childlike *naïveté*; and if the mind from which they flow draws its sources from the inexhaustible fountain of beauty, they will possess all the charms of virginity. Mozart might be named as the representative genius of this kind of delightfully fresh spontaneity. Unfortunately, the times of juvenile enjoyment have been changed for the manhood of deeper thought and sorrow. We have tasted the bitter fruit of knowledge, and the artists of our latter days must have passed with us through the furnace of "fierce and unfathomable thought," purifying in it the inarticulate longings of the soul, to the not less passionate but conscious strife for ideal aims. Beethoven and Wagner are the artists by whose names the philosophical, and therefore essentially modern, epoch of music will be recognised. By these remarks, however, it shall by no means be implied that the works of Wagner or Beethoven are not the emanation of spontaneous production, but have been fashioned after a certain scheme, the result of previous speculation. In Wagner's case the futility of such an accusation can easily be proved by chronological dates. He himself has told us how "unintentionally" (*unvorsätzlich*) he entered upon his career as a reformer in the *Flying Dutchman*. This work, *Tannhäuser*, and *Lohengrin* were finished, and even the scheme of the words of *Siegfried* and the *Meistersinger* conceived and partly executed, before his first theoretical work, the

Kunstwerk der Zukunft, saw the light. It is indeed one of the most interesting studies of musical history to see how the new idea in all its consequences grew upon Wagner, and how he embodied it unconsciously in his dramatic creations, which only afterwards, like the works of any other composer, served him as material for his researches. The great importance of these theoretic writings lies, for us, in the fact of their being the only way in which a full understanding of Wagner's aims, and further, of those of modern music in general, can be obtained.

Germany is the country of music and philosophy, but the philosophy of music has been treated by most of its deepest thinkers with an undeserved and equally unaccountable neglect. Even a man of Leibnitz's pre-eminence saw in music only an " exercitium arithmeticæ occultum nescientis se numerare animi," although the works of his contemporaries, Bach and Handel, might have taught him better. Hegel's views on the same subject cannot be said to enlighten the mind to any considerable extent, and in our own time Friedrich Vischer, the *"Aesthetiker" par excellence*, confessed his own ignorance of music in a double way, first by not treating it himself in his principal work, and secondly by choosing Dr. Hanslick as his substitute. Arthur Schopenhauer, the greatest thinker Germany has produced since Kant, was the first to pierce the clouds hanging around this most ethereal art. There is a certain likeness between the characters of Wagner and Schopenhauer as writers, and equally between the positions which they take in the history of their respective branches of human development. Both acknowledge one and only one, of their predecessors as their superior, whose ideas they are destined to carry out. In this exclusive admiration of Beethoven and Kant, on the part of Wagner and Schopenhauer, lies at the same time the cause for their frequently unjust contempt of epigonic aspirations and the bitterness of their critical utterances. Perhaps such one-sidedness and misunderstanding of individualities not strictly akin to their own is inevitably the doom of creative minds; but only too often it leads to a fatal isolation from the stream of contemporary progress. The bitter resentment on the part of the objects concerned is another disadvantage of such reformatory zeal. The flaying of Marsyas, —wretched singer though he may have been,— seemed to me always the least enviable part of

Apollo's career. In both Wagner's and Schopenhauer's cases the numerous victims of their wrath agreed upon a system of self-defence and revenge, in which the positive and negative weapons of abuse, and even more pernicious silence, were handled with considerable skill, and the temporary success of which showed the influential position of the Marsyas tribe in the literary community. The consequence was, that of Schopenhauer's standard work scarcely two editions were sold in almost half a century, while the immense importance of Wagner's ideas is only just now, after a painful struggle of more than thirty years, beginning to dawn upon his own nation. It is perhaps partly owing to this affinity of character that Wagner adopted, with slight modifications, the great pessimist's views on the ideal basis of music. Into Schopenhauer's views, as contained in 'The World as Will and Imagination,' we therefore now must enter a little more fully.

The great discovery of Kant, in the 'Critique of Pure Reason,' is the doctrine that the outer world, or what we call the universe, appeals to our senses only by means of its *phenomenon*. About the real essence, the *noumenon* of this world, as it might appear to beings with other means of perception than ours, and not limited by the notions of space and time, nothing is revealed to us. Even these notions originate, according to Kant, in a certain predisposition of the brain, by means of which we discern the co-existence and succession of different phenomena and the phenomena themselves. Against the absolute idealism of Berkeley, Kant holds that, outside the human Ego, there must exist an independent *something* to act upon the individual. Schopenhauer, starting from this basis, proceeds to the further assertion that this something hitherto nondescript exists only in so far as it has the "will of existence;" in fact, that it is nothing else but this will in its different forms and phases. The highest and last of these phases is the human volition, made conscious of its being and aims by the intellect, and comprising in its microcosm the universe out of which it grows, and from which it differs gradually but not essentially. The first manifestation of this will, Schopenhauer proceeds, takes place in the ideas in Plato's sense, —that is, in the archetypal forms which fashion the cosmos, and of which the single phenomena are further subdivisions. It is the aim of all arts to express the eternal essence of things by means of these Platonic ideas, only music takes in this respect an exceptional position. Arts like painting and sculpture embody these ideas, as conceived by the artist through the medium of phenomena, the ideal value of which he shows, but only by the reproduction of their actual appearance. Even in poetry the realities of life and the visible wonders of the world, with their symbolic meaning, form an essential ingredient. Music, on the contrary, does not want, nor even allow of, a realistic conception. There is no sound in nature fit to serve the musician as a model, or to supply him with more than an occasional suggestion for his sublime ' purpose. He approaches the original sources of existence more closely than all other artists—nay, even than Nature herself. His harmonies and melodies are, to speak with Schopenhauer, "as immediate and direct an objectification or copy of the will of the world as the world itself is, as the ideas are of which the universe of things is the phenomenon. Music is not the copy of the ideas, like the other arts, but a representation of the cosmical will co-ordinate with the ideas themselves." In this sense the musical composer is the only *creative* artist. While the painter or sculptor must borrow the raiment for his idea from the human form or the landscape, the musician is alone with his inspiration. He only listens to the voice of the spirit of the world, or, which is the same, of his own spirit speaking to him as in a dream; for it is only in dreams, when the soul is not disturbed by the impression of the senses, that such a state of absorption is attainable, and Vogl's saying of Schubert, that he composed in a state of *clairvoyance*, may be applied to all creative musicians.

These are, in brief, the fundamental principles which Schopenhauer, first among philosophers, has laid down for the metaphysical essence of our art, and which Wagner has adopted, without any modifications of importance, in his lately published pamphlet on Beethoven.

It ought, however, to be added that in the final conclusions with regard to the concrete appearances of musical genius, which both the artist and philosopher have founded on this common basis, they differ widely. Schopenhauer seems to have considered music as an art of entirely independent and self-sufficient means of expression, the free movement of which could only suffer from a too close alliance with worded poetry. He even goes to the length of highly commending Rossini's way of proceeding, in which the words of the text are treated quite *en bagatelle*, and in which, therefore, "music speaks its own language so purely and distinctly that it does not require the words at all, and has its full effect even if performed by instruments only." Such a sentence cannot but surprise us from the same lips, which have uttered the profound thoughts referred to on the foregoing pages. But the philosopher has that in common with the poet, that his abstract contemplations arise from an intuitive consciousness, which is all but independent of, and not always applicable to, the results of actual knowledge.

The philosophical side of the question being thus stated, we have now to follow Wagner on his own grounds, in order to witness the bearing of this speculation on the historical progress of our art. The theoretical works of Wagner, to the contents of which I wish to introduce the reader in the next following pages, are considerable in number and variety of subject-matter. In glancing through the complete edition of his writings, lately published in nine volumes, one is struck with admiration at the range of an intellectual power which, greatly exceeding the limits of one art, lays a firm hold on almost all the moving currents of contemporary thought, overpowering their heterogeneous motions, and leading them with an unequalled force of concentration to the one aim of its own aspiration. Politics, religion, history, and national economy are treated with the same sovereign power of centripetal rotation, in so far as they may tend to the desired ideal of a new phase of art, and of national and individual life regenerated through means of it. For the artist is to be the longed-for Messiah, to deliver future generations from the fetters of custom and prejudice, and I need not add that this artist is to speak to the nations from the hallowed boards of a truly popular stage, and that his words shall be accompanied by the inspiring strains of the divinest of arts, *music*. "Rebus humanis inest quidam circulus," we may exclaim with the great Roman historian, when, in this boldest dream of our latter days, we perceive a close affinity to the Greek drama and its vital reciprocity with the life of the nation; an affinity which, as we shall see hereafter, even extends to the internal economy of this drama and its two most important compounds.

It would, of course, lead us too far to follow Wagner's thought into all its collateral ramifications. The present writer will think himself happy if he should succeed, in condensing into an organic whole the abundance of speculative material, as far as it relates more immediately to the subject in point, *i.e.*, the relative positions of music and poetry in their united efforts.

2.

From the entirely supernatural character of music as established by Schopenhauer, Wagner proceeds to conclude its comparative independence of the conditions under which the visible world acts upon our senses; that is, of space and time. In an art of sound, space is altogether out of the question; but even time can in a certain sense be dispensed with in what is most musical in music—harmony. A harmonic chord, as such, is absolutely unmeasurable by time; and in pieces, like the divine works of Palestrina, where the gradual progress from one harmonious combination to another is scarcely perceptible, the consciousness of change, and with it that of passing time itself, almost ceases, and we seem to have entered, under the master's guidance, the quiet realms of divine non-existence. But music could not always remain in this state of passive calm, and as soon as its other most important element, rhythm, is introduced, everything changes suddenly, and we are at once transported into the restless waves of time and progress. For, as we know from Aristoxenos, rhythm is nothing but a regular return of shorter and longer portions of time, as manifested by a movement performed in this time, the object of the movement in music being the succession of melodious intervals—*i.e.*, the μέλος, or tune. Melody, therefore, is the daughter of the quiet repose in harmony and the throbbing motion of rhythm, and both elements are equally necessary for its beautiful growth. Still, rhythm being an intruder in the realm of pure music, the compositions which, like dances, are exclusively founded on it must be of a lower order than where the melody grows out of harmonious relations. With these three elements, viz., harmony, rhythm, and melody, we have exhausted the means of expression which music proper can call its own. Also about its aims and objects there can be no doubt, after the foregoing remarks. Music's own domain is the reign of unimpaired impulse,—the tenderest vibrations of will and passion,—as the immediate effluence of which we have to consider it. But its origin, as well as the character of its instruments, excludes it from the sphere of actual realities, and prevents it from rivalling articulate speech in the distinct rendering of emotions.

The purest and most adequate organ of our art in its independent state, is instrumental music, the separate existence of which is of comparatively recent date, beginning with Bach, and ending (if we may believe Wagner) with Beethoven's Ninth Symphony. In this, even the supreme genius of Beethoven confesses its inability of expressing its highest aspiration in music alone; it calls poetry to its assistance, and the words of Schiller's 'Freude,' added to Beethoven's enchanted strains, sound, as it were, the deathknell of music in its separate condition, and the rise of a new epoch, in which music and poetry can be severed no more. With this view we are able to agree only in a modified way, but will not at present interrupt the progress of Wagner's ideas by untimely deviation. The combination of music and poetry, Wagner proceeds, to which Beethoven repaired when the insufficiency of his musical means became obvious, was of course not invented or used for the first time by him. It, on the contrary, preceded the artificial separation of the two arts. The traditions of all nations speak of the poet and singer as the same person, and the mere fact of the human voice being at the same time one of the most perfect musical instruments, seems to indicate the organic necessity of such a combination, as divined in the lines of the 'Passionate Pilgrim '—

> "If music and sweet poetry agree
> As they must needs, the sister and the brother.
>   *   *   *
> One God is God of both as poets feign."

Besides, the metrical element which exists in an embryonic and all but latent state in the spoken language, can be interpreted and displayed in all its charms only by the aid of real melody, which, as it were, must grow out of the rhythmical structure of verse and stanza. In their ideal aims the two sister arts form also a necessary complement to each other. The free expression of intense and abundant feeling in poetry is but too often encumbered by the speculative structure of language, while, on the other hand, the soaring flight of music, lacks a starting-point of strictly defined and recognisable pathos. Music and poetry, therefore, by both their powers and weaknesses are referred to each other's aid; and the results of their combination will be of a higher order than is attainable by either of them in their separate state. On the other hand, it cannot be denied that their close union will be made possible only by a mutual compromise, in which either of them has to resign certain peculiarities of its own in favour of the common aim.

The way in which such a compromise has been attempted has varied considerably in different times and nations. In the lyrical parts of the Greek tragedy (for it is to the drama, as the highest result of both music and poetry, that we have now to turn our chief attention), music, as we know, took a prominent part; so prominent, indeed, that the metrical structure of the choric pieces can be understood only from its connection with song. This importance appears in a still stronger light, if with Professor Nietzsche,* we consider music in the antique drama as the representative of the *Bacchic* element which forms the wild ecstatic undercurrent of the measured *Apollonian* self-consciousness of the spoken dialogue, and in this way becomes the symbol of that most mysterious phase of Greek and, in a wider sense, of human nature. Still the essentially rhythmical nature of Greek composition could not be favourable to the flow of melody, which, as we have seen, depends for its more elevated effects chiefly on harmonious beauty. Unfortunately the sense for harmony seems to have been little in accordance with the other accomplishments of the most artistic nation of the world. Even if we follow the most favourable accounts, the knowledge of polyphony was all but wanting among the Greeks, and the imperfect nature of their scales, without the major seventh, betrays, at least according to our notions, a deplorable want of musical ear. Under these circumstances it scarcely required the powers of Æschylus or Sophocles to

* In his interesting work, *Die Geburt der Tragödie aus dem Geiste der Musik* (The Birth of the Tragedy from the Spirit of Music). Leipsic: Fritzsch.

c 2

settle the question of preponderance in the Greek tragedy in favour of poetry, which had all the advantages of technical perfection in the hands of men of unmatchable genius. It remains to acknowledge the keen perception of the relations of the two arts shown by the Greeks in this treatment, in which music, imperfect though it might be, was applied to its true purpose of intensifying the rhythmical power and ideal pathos of words.

This state of things was entirely changed in the next important phase of dramatic music which we encounter in Italy, about the beginning of the seventeenth century. Like the renaissance of the fine arts, the Italian opera was, or pretended to be, a revival of antique traditions. But the affinity between the two epochs in regard to this was of a very superficial character. Music this time entered the lists under much more favourable auspices. First of all, the language it had to deal with had lost its rhythmical character entirely; in poetry a mere counting of syllables had taken the place of metrical accentuation, and music was at full liberty to supply the want of arsis and thesis according to its own conditions. The character of modern feeling was likewise more akin to the intense, but vague and indistinct nature of musical expression. In its way through the middle ages, with their romantic conception of love, and the mysterious terrors and charms of Christian revelation, mankind had lost that firm grasp of realities which always formed the substratum of the loftiest flights of Greek genius. There were certain vibrations of feeling in this longing for the supernatural which would not allow of the limits of words, and absolutely required the more congenial raiment of pure sound. At the epoch we speak of the great poets of Italy had passed away, and the void which had been left even by their mighty deeds now remained to be filled up by the musician, whose means were by this time more equal to his great task. For his art had now passed out of the stage of childish stammering. The homophonous innocence of the Doric and Mixolydic scales had left only a dim tradition. Polyhymnia had undergone the uncouth attempts at discipline which we are used to attribute to Hucbald. She had learnt from Guittone di Arezzo to fix her thoughts in indelible signs, and two centuries' training in the school of the Netherlands had taught her the powers of polyphonous figuration. When this school reached its climax in the great Orlando di Lasso, and in Goudimel's pupil, the divine Roman, Palestrina, music had not to shun comparison with any of the sister arts.

The superior position which it was thus enabled to take could not be favourable to its harmonious co-operation with poetry in the result of their combined efforts—the opera. It is true that at the beginning the rights of music were asserted in a very modest way. In the first lyrical drama, 'Daphnis,' which was performed at Florence, in 1594, the musical part seems to have consisted chiefly in the transformation of the spoken dialogue into recitative, both of the "secco" and "obligato" kinds, accompanied by the orchestra, such as it was at the time. But Monteverde soon afterwards became bolder in his musical conceptions. Both the orchestral and vocal parts were increased by the introduction of so-called symphonies (*i.e.*, preludes and interludes), and ensemble pieces for the singers. Alessandro Scarlatti first used the regular form of the aria in the opera, which henceforth became entirely dependent on musical purposes. Certain established forms of absolute music, like finale or duet, were bodily transferred into the action of the piece, without any regard to their poetical propriety. In the course of time the poet became the bondsman of the musician, and had to arrange his *libretti* (as they were ignominiously called) entirely according to the arbitrary decision of the latter. Even the human voice, the last stronghold of the poetical element in music, was treated henceforth like any other instrument, only with a view to display its beauties of sound. In most cases it seems as if words were put into the mouth of the singer only as more convenient for him to pronounce than meaningless vowels. At most their contents served to give the composer some slight indication whether to write a brilliant allegro or a languid adagio. Nearly the same might be said of the whole dramatic poem, the merits of which depended almost entirely on its adaptedness for musical purposes. The dulness and absurdity of most of these productions are, in consequence, almost inconceivable. Soon, however, music in its own sphere had to experience the evil results of this neglect of its natural foundation. Forgetful of its higher artistic aims, it lost hold of all poetic meaning, and was degraded to a mere display of skill on the part of clever vocalists, who performed the most daring *salti mortali* on the tight-rope of *fioriture*. If formerly the composer had encroached upon the domain of the poet, he now on his part was made the slave of the *castrato*, who, with great real merit as a vocal virtuoso, combined an innocence of all artistic intentions scarcely to be equalled even by the stars of the modern operatic stage.

It was against this omnipotence of the singer that the great German composers protested when they took up the barren forms of the Italian opera, and filled them with new vitality. Mozart was one of the first of a brilliant group of dramatic composers to take the lead in this crusade against Italian artificiality. He was endowed by nature with the richest gift of musical productiveness that ever was possessed by man, and it is no wonder that the genuine touches of nature and dramatic pathos which we still admire after the lapse of nearly a century, acted as a wholesome antidote on the spirits of his contemporaries against the soporific effects of Hesperic vocalisation. Still, Mozart's genius was too decidedly of a musical character to attempt, or even wish for, an operatic reform on the basis of poetry. To him also the opera appeared, like the symphony or sonata, as an entirely musical formation, in which the addition of poetry seemed only of importance as suggesting opportunities for the display of the powers of his own art. He would never have approved of the slightest concession of musical prerogative in favour of dramatic economy. Take, for instance, the scene in *Figaro* where the page is hidden in the closet of the Countess, and her husband, mad with jealousy at finding the door locked, rushes away for the necessary instruments to make his entrance by force. As soon as he is out of sight, Cherubino appears, and seeing no other way of saving his life and the honour of his mistress, is about to jump out of window. There is *periculum in mora*, and a moment's delay may be of fatal consequence. But here Mozart saw the opportunity for an effective piece of music. Cherubino and Susanna begin their duet, and fate, in the shape of the Count with his hammer and drawn sword, has to wait at the door till *tonic* and *dominant* have had their due. The admirable way in which the anxiety of the situation is rendered by Mozart's music cannot atone for this interruption of the dramatic action. The mere fact of his introducing a piece of music in the distinct form of a duet at such a moment shows Mozart's inability for the post of a dramatic Messiah, as which he is still considered by many of his blind worshippers.

Neither can we be surprised at seeing Mozart adopt the whole apparatus of the *opera seria*. It was not in his tender and unpolemical nature to destroy established forms with the sword of the reformer; he could only make us forget the narrowness of these fetters. His great merit for the development of dramatic music consists in his having shown and increased its capability of rendering poetic intention. Of the greatest importance for us is the fact that even he was not able to write beautiful and impressive music to dull and unsuggestive words. The comparison with this view, of *La Clemenza di Tito* and *Don Giovanni*, or of *Cosi fan Tutte* and *Figaro*, proves more clearly than any philosophical argument could do that music, even in the hands of a Mozart, depends for its highest effects on the assistance of its sister art. "And so," Wagner says, "it would have been Mozart, the most absolute of all musicians, who would have solved the problem of the opera long ago; that is, who would have assisted in producing the truest, the most beautiful, and most perfect *drama*, if he had met with a poet whom he as a musician would only have had to *assist*. But such a poet he unfortunately was never to find." This quotation may serve at the same time as a test of veracity on the part of Wagner's enemies, who persistently accuse him of defiling the name of Mozart, and of erecting from the scattered ruins of his rival's fame the column of his own glory.

Very different from Mozart's unpremeditated and entirely spontaneous effort is the way in which Gluck approached the problem of settling the balance between music and poetry in the opera. The tendency of his works was of a decidedly reformatory character, and the principle which he carried out in his music, and to which he gave utterance even in words, was, that the task of dramatic music is, and is only, to accompany the different phases of emotion indicated in the text, and that its position to worded poetry is therefore of a subordinate kind. In this way the immoderate influence of the singer was made impossible for evermore ; he was henceforth to be the mouthpiece of the poet, and consequently had to take the greatest possible care in conveying the full poetical meaning of his song to the audience. By this means the declamatory element became of the highest importance for the composer as well as the performer, and the recitative, in which this element finds its fullest expression, was brought by Gluck to an unequalled degree of perfection. A further progress marked by his reform is the greater consideration paid to the dramatic economy of the libretti. Frequent and continued interruption of the action by an uncalled-for display of musical powers was made all but impossible. The revolutionising tendency of our composer was felt keenly by the adherents of the old system, and the hatred of the two parties became evident when their two champions, Piccini and Gluck, met face to face on the battle-field of the stage. The scene of their deadly contest was the gay Paris of 1777, and the ardour with which it was carried on was quite worthy of the important questions at stake. The highest ranks of French literature and society, royalty itself not excluded, became partisans of the Italian or Franco-German *gonfalonière*.

In order to understand the reason why men of the intellectual eminence of Laharpe, Diderot, and at least for a certain time Rousseau himself, fought on what we now call the conservative or rather the retrograde side, it will be required to enter to some extent into the origin of a struggle which reached its climax at the above-mentioned time, but the deeper causes of which date back to a much earlier period. I hope that the historical interest attaching to the antagonists, no less than the importance of the questions at stake, will make the reader find a short deviation from my immediate subject excusable. The national style of the opera railed at by the *Italianissimi*, and extolled with equal emphasis by the frequenters of the "coin de la reine,"* was not originally a product of French soil. Lully, who may be considered its father, was of Italian birth (Florence, 1633), but brought up in France, where he also received his first musical training. He composed no less than nineteen operas and twenty-six divertissements and ballets, mostly for the court festivities of Louis the Fourteenth. His friendly relations to Molière are

* So called from the gentlemen of the queen's court taking their seats in that particular corner of the theatre and forming the nucleus of the anti-Italian party. The queen herself —the unfortunate Marie-Antoinette—took a lively interest in the fates of the French opera, and particularly in those of her compatriot Gluck.

known to the student of literature. The exclusive privilege of performing operas in Paris was granted to him, and by the permanent establishment in this way of the so-called *Académie Royale de Musique*, the foundation was laid of a school of dramatic composers, which, whatever its merits or demerits may have been, at least can lay claim to possessing an unmistakable type of its own. True to the declamatory spirit of French dramatic art, Lully had modelled his style to a great extent after the earlier form of the Italian opera, in which, as we have seen, the recitative played a prominent part, adding, however, a greater variety of concerted and orchestral pieces, in accordance with the more advanced stage of music at his time. The splendour of scenic effects and courtly pageants formed another important attraction of his fashionable entertainments. The course thus begun was continued by Lully's most celebrated follower, Rameau (1683-1764), whose mode of expression cannot be said to differ essentially from that of his great predecessor, making allowances, however, for individual peculiarities and the progress of musical art in general. The comparative merits of the two composers are expounded by Rousseau in the usual forcible and lucid style of that great writer. His evidence is the more valuable, as his impartiality between the two is warranted by the fact of his being their common adversary in the contest of Italian *v.* French music. " One must confess," he says, " that M. Rameau possesses very great talent, much fire and euphony, and a considerable knowledge of harmonious combinations and effects ; one also must grant him the art of appropriating the ideas of others, by changing their character, adorning and developing them, and turning them round in all manner of ways. On the other hand he shows less facility of inventing new ones ; altogether he has more skill than fertility, more knowledge than genius, or rather genius smothered by knowledge, but always force, grace, and very often a beautiful *cantilena.* His recitative is not as natural but much more varied than that of Lully; admirable in a few scenes, but bad as a rule. He was the first to write symphonies and rich accompaniments." Rousseau continues by reproaching Rameau with a too powerful instrumentation, compared with Italian simplicity, and adds, summing up, that nobody had better understood than Rameau, to conceive the spirit of single passages, and to produce artistic contrasts, but that he entirely failed in giving to his operas " a happy and much to be desired unity." In another part of the quoted passage Rousseau says, that Rameau stands far beneath Lully as far as *esprit* and artistic tact are concerned, but that he is often superior to him in his mode of dramatic expression.

The chief objections raised by our philosopher against the French opera, besides the overloaded instrumentation alluded to, are the monotony of its modulations, the frequency of perfect cadences as necessitated by its declamatory character, and what Rousseau calls the separation of its melody from the language.

His remarks as to the last point show a depth of thought with regard to the fundamental principles of music which, particularly at the period when they were written, would surprise us but for the sublime greatness of the intellect from which they sprang.

The gist of the following passage tallies too well with what we shall have to say of Wagner's ideas about the innate melody of languages, not to make its quotation excusable: "J'ai dit que toute musique nationale tire son principal caractère de la langue qui lui est propre, et je dois ajouter que c'est principalement la prosodie de la langue qui constitue ce caractère. Comme la musique vocale a précédé de beaucoup l'instrumentale, celle-ci a toujours reçu de l'autre ses tours de chant et sa mesure ; et les diverses mesures de la musique vocale n'ont pu naître, que des diverses manières dont on pouvait scander le discours et placer les brèves et les longues, les unes à l'égard des autres : ce qui est très évident dans la musique Grecque, dont toutes les mesures n'étaient que les formules d'autant de rhythmes fournis par tous les arrangements des syllabes longues ou brèves, et des pieds dont la langue et la poésie étaient susceptibles." In quite agreeing with what Rousseau on various occasions says about the rhythmical deficiencies of French prosody, one can, on the other hand, not but be astonished at his looking for help in this respect to the Italian language, in which the force of metrical accentuation has entirely dissolved itself into sonorous beauty, and which, moreover, was treated by operatic composers in their arias and *recitativi secchi* with the utmost *nonchalance*. We are here again reminded of the peculiar gift of great philosophic intellects, of establishing, by dint of intuitive speculation, axioms of an independent, and sometimes much higher kind, than their authors' individual opinions on particular subjects would lead to expect. In Rousseau's case, however, psychological reasons for his strange predilection are not absent. First of all he loved Italy and its beautiful language with the love of a poet. It can, also, not be denied that the easy melodiousness of Pergolese and Jomelli was decidedly of superior attraction, compared with the dignified but somewhat monotonous pathos of 'Tancrède' and 'Hippolyte et Aricie.' Moreover, the Académie Royale was an institution of acknowledged excellence and imbued with all the arrogant superciliousness of an established reputation. On hearing the cynical nephew of Rameau* talking of the "big wigs assembling every Friday these thirty or forty years," or of his uncle, "le grand Rameau," walking in the Tuileries garden with his hands folded on his back, and frowning down on the world in general from the sublime height of his glory, one can quite understand why men of genius turned restive and

---

* In Diderot's witty pamphlet, 'Le Neveu de Rameau.'

praised the rivalling *Bouffons* from a mere spirit of opposition. In justice to Rousseau, it ought to be added that when Gluck himself appeared on the stage as the French champion, he willingly acknowledged the great composer's genius. In a letter to Dr. Burney, written shortly before his death, Rousseau gives a close and appreciative analysis of the German master's *Alceste*, the first Italian version of which Gluck had submitted to him for suggestions; and when on the first performance of the piece not being received favourably by the Parisian audience, the composer exclaimed, "*Alceste* est tombée," Rousseau is said to have comforted him with the flattering *bon mot*, "Oui, mais elle est tombée du ciel."

The affinity between Gluck's aspirations and the French national opera was to a considerable extent of a negative kind. It consisted chiefly in his strongly opposing the encroachments of mere vocal skill on the domain of dramatic truth, as represented by the Italian *opera seria*. The bearing of his reformatory act became the more impressive as he was prepared to urge its necessity with the full consciousness of æsthetical speculation. "Je chercherai," he says in his celebrated dedication of 'Alceste' to the

Grand Duke of Tuscany, "à reduire la musique à sa veritable fonction, celle de seconder la poésie pour fortifier l'expression des sentiments et l'intérêt des situations, sans interrompre l'action et la refroidir par des ornements superflus." This programme might almost literally be adopted by the disciples of the modern school, and the reproaches aimed by the conservatives at what was then the music of the future also remind one curiously of the critical utterances of which Wagner has been and is still the enviable object. But beyond this capability of raising the indignant alarm of critical worthies, the artistic consequences of Gluck's and Wagner's works have not as much in common as is generally believed. It is true that Gluck already felt the necessity of a perfect unity between music and poetry, but he never intended to bring about this desirable effect by surrendering any of the strict forms of his own art. The consequence was that the poet was even more bound to adapt his work to the intentions of the composer, and that the latter remained practically the omnipotent ruler on the operatic stage.

The high condition of the contemporary spoken drama in France had been of considerable influence on Gluck's production. He wrote or re-wrote his most important works for the opera in Paris and to French words; we cannot therefore be surprised at discerning the immediate results of his career more distinctly in France than in his native country. The grand opera in Paris was swayed for a long time by the great German maestro's traditions, as continued by a school of highly accomplished artists. The representative names of this school are Méhul, Cherubini, and Spontini (the latter two, although Italian by birth, living quite under the mighty spell of French nationality in the same degree as we have seen it repeated in our own days in Meyerbeer and Offenbach), whose place in the history of their art will be secured for ever, by the additional dramatic power and intensity which music owes to their efforts. Still the traditional encumbrances of poetical development by the established musical forms remained unshaken by them.

To those mentioned already, we have now to add two more attempts at the regeneration of the opera made at almost the same time in two different countries. Italy, the old cradle of the divine art, was to recover once more her position at the head of musical Europe. Rossini, the most gifted and most spoiled of her sons, sallied forth with an innumerable army of bacchantic melodies to conquer the world, the Messiah of joy, the breaker of thought and sorrow. Europe by this time had got tired of the pompous seriousness of French declamation. It lent but too willing an ear to the new gospel, and eagerly quaffed the intoxicating potion which Rossini poured out in inexhaustible streams. Looking back with calmer eyes at the enormous enthusiasm with which, Rossini was received by our grandfathers, we are almost at a loss to discern the causes for such an unequalled success. It requires, indeed, all the patience of an English audience to endure nowadays a performance of *Otello*, *Semiramide*, or any of Rossini's serious operas except *Gillaume Tell*. The *recitativo secco* is treated by him with all the dryness which this ominous name implies. The melodious structure, mostly founded on dance-like rhythms, verges constantly on the trivial, and wherever Rossini covets the forbidden fruit of counterpoint, his deficiencies become sadly obvious. Only rarely the swan of Pesaro rises with the dramatic power of the situation to a remarkable height of passionate impulse. But Rossini knew his public, and he knew equally well his own resources; prudent, as most Italians are, he did his best to profit by the chances of the situation. What he could do and did admirably well was to open the rich mines of melodious beauty with which nature had endowed him, and which it is so easy to augment and develop in a country whose very language is music, and where the *gondolieri* chant the stanzas of Tasso to self-invented tunes. This principle of absolute melodiousness, as Rossini carried it out to its extreme, combined with the charming freshness of his good-natured humour, was well adapted to silence the objections of graver criticism in the universal uproar of popular applause. The unpleasant fact of a strong family likeness among all these sweet children of song and their common mother the waltz, whether they deplored the sad fate of Desdemona or mimicked the jealous rage of the Seville Dottore, seems to have struck only very few of the enchanted hearers. We need scarcely add that the pretended reform of dramatic music on the basis of Rossini's absolute melody was a total failure in all respects.

Almost contemporary with his great success, and to a certain extent in opposition to it, we have to record another movement of operatic development much purer in its artistic aims and very different in its lasting consequences. Karl Maria von Weber stood at the head of this movement, which took its rise from the strong romantic and national feeling pervading at the time all the ranks of German society and literature. It is a remarkable fact that the composer of *Der Freischütz* had also supplied with their musical garment the war songs of Körner and Schenkendorf, which roused and expressed the patriotic indignation against the yoke of the foreign oppressor. Closely connected with this national elevation was the revival of mediæval and popular poetry with its sweet odour of forest and meadow, and all this Weber now embodied in his dramatic creations. By this, the first essentially new and highly important addition was made to the resources of the opera, as Mozart left it. Rossini's cantilena, although sparkling with originality, was in form and essence nothing but an exact reproduction of the Italian aria of the last century. Weber's melody, on the contrary, was founded entirely on the tune of the *Volkslied*, and to its close connection with the inexhaustible and ever new creating power of popular feeling, it owed the charm of its delightful freshness. Every passion and sentiment within the range of this pure and simple language Weber expressed with incomparable beauty; only where the grand pathos of dramatic action demands a higher scope of musical conception the limits of his power become obvious. For the foundation of his dramatic production after all was melody, melody quite as absolute, although much purer and nobler than that of Rossini; and the ultimate harmonious amalgamation of music and poetry, by which alone a pure dramatic effect is attainable, was not to be found on this basis.

The new element of national and popular colouring in music was soon appreciated in all its practical results by Weber's skilful colleagues of the French operatic stage. The versatile genius of Rossini proved equal to the occasion. Full of the new idea, he left his country, crossed the Alps, and entered triumphantly the capital of modern civilisation laden with the *Ranz des Vaches* and other melodious specimens of the Alpine flora, the innocent charms of which he was to interpret to the *habitués* of the Grand Opera. Auber, with a simultaneous impulse, explored the Gulf of

Naples, and embodied the results of his Lazzaroni experience in the immortal melodies of the *Muette de Portici*. The climax of this national, or as it has also been called, historic phase of the opera was reached by Meyerbeer, Weber's countryman and co-disciple of Abbate Vogler. He was too well acquainted with the mysterious practices of popular effect, not to see at a glance the immense advantages of a striking air of the national kind. Reverence for the historic individuality of such a tune, and the movement represented by it, was something entirely strange to his eclectic turn of mind; witness the sacrilegious way in which he treated Luther's monumental hymn in the *Huguenots*, with all the *raffinement* of the French opera. His artistic conscience was never troubled while he was safe (as well he might be) that his trick would not be found out by the compatriots of his selection. While fully agreeing with Wagner's severe condemnation of such unprincipled writing for momentary effect, by which Meyerbeer degraded his own genius and that of his art, we cannot help saying that, upon the whole, his opinion of the composer of the *Huguenots* seems to be marked by an unjustifiable severity. Dramatic music owes to Meyerbeer new accents of genuine pathos, which have added considerably to its powers of rendering passionate emotions. Wagner's aversion seems to find its psychological explanation to a certain extent in the circumstance, that his own first efforts moved in the sphere of Meyerbeer and Halévi, and that from his present higher point of view he looks back with intense horror on the sins of his youth.

Surveying once more the different stages through which we have accompanied the opera, from its modest beginning in the sixteenth century to the present day, we notice an enormous progress in the variety and intensity of its means of expression, but scarcely any change in the relative position of poetry and music, of which the latter was from beginning to end considered as the sovereign principle imposing its own conditions on the sister art. The problem of a harmonious union of the two elements could not, as we have seen, be solved on this unnatural basis.

We might call it a kind of Nemesis that in the highest development of music in its separate existence, in the symphony, the demand of a previous poetic inspiration was felt at first, and that it was Beethoven, the greatest musical creator

of all times, who was to bow down before the
eternal rights of poetry, and usher in the new
epoch of what we still may call the music of the
future. It must be confessed that before him his
art had been in a state of unconsciousness of its
own powers and duties. None of the great composers had taken a higher aim than that of displaying the beauties of music in its own limits, that is,
in the domain of sound. Hence the wonderful
variety of melodious and harmonious combinations
in the old Italian masters; hence the prodigious
skill in the polyphonous texture of Bach's and
Handel's counterpoint. The growth and climax
of emotions which these beautiful sounds might
convey to the mind remained a secondary consideration, and wherever such emotions were
condensed into words, their divergence from the
accompanying music was not always avoided by
the greatest masters. The motive of the opening
chorus, for instance, in Bach's celebrated cantata,
'Ich hatte viel Bekümmerniss,' would suit a joyous
ditty quite as well as the quoted complaint of a
sorrowful Christian. Perhaps in many cases Bach
had sketched the theme of his fugue before he chose
the corresponding words. Examples of the same in-

congruity might be quoted from all the standard works of the last century—Gluck's operas not excluded. It was, in fact, unavoidable as long as the musical conception preceded in time and importance the poetical idea, whether or not expressed in distinct words. Not so in Beethoven. In all the bliss of musical creation he betrays a longing for something of which he himself was scarcely aware, but which he descried with the unconscious divination of genius, and the marks of which are traceable in the works of his last and grandest period. He was the first to condense the vague feelings which were all that music had hitherto expressed into more distinctly intelligible ideas. He even brings the song of birds, the thunder, and the murmuring brook before the ear, not as a portrait of nature, but as at once a suggestion and embodiment of the feelings which would be called up by them; *Mehr Ausdruck der Empfindung als Malerei*, as he wrote himself at the head of his Pastoral Symphony. In Schopenhauer's parallel between the act of composing and a dream, this phase of Beethoven's artistic creation would represent the transition between sleeping and waking, where the recovering senses supply the mind with images from the outer world to clothe its dream, which was naked and shapeless. Indeed, there are passages in Beethoven's later instrumental works, such as long distinct recitativi, which can only be explained by the presence of some occult idea struggling for self-consciousness, or, if it may be, expression. This idea being previous to all musical conception, the forms of absolute music had to submit to its harmonious expansion, and in this way the spell of their unlimited sway was broken for ever. It therefore was Beethoven who restored the true relations of the two arts, which henceforth became inseparable. The possibility of music for the sole sake of sonorous beauty has virtually ceased to exist, and any composer with higher aspirations than those of a *genre* painter, without subject or artistic purpose, has to consider it his task to express a preconceived poetical idea by means of his sound. It is the part of music to receive this idea, and to bring it forth again idealised and raised to its own sphere of pure passion. "For music," as Wagner beautifully expresses it, "is a *woman;* the essence of a woman's nature is love, but this love is receptive, and surrendering itself unconditionally to the beloved.

The result of Beethoven's gigantic reform for the opera is at once visible. Music in its new position could never attempt to fetter the organic growth of the drama by imposing upon it conditions strange to its own nature. Henceforth the art of sound was limited to its own sphere of intensifying the poet's conceptions by means of its ideal powers. It was not given to Beethoven himself, to make the one last step to the music-drama, perhaps only because he did not find a poem congenial to his inspiration. But it was he who showed the capability of music for this task not by his single opera, which belongs to an early period of his career, and, after all, is not more than a symphony of instruments and human voices, but by the works of his last period, and foremost of all by his Ninth Symphony, the sublime accompaniment of some immense drama, of which mankind itself, with all its doubts, pains, and joys, is the hero. Wagner calls the Ninth Symphony the last that was ever written, and seems to deny the possibility of a further progress of music except in its dramatic sphere. With this, however, we are obliged to disagree to some extent. The music-drama is certainly the highest type of musical development;

still, the emergence of this does not make impossible or irrational the perpetuation and perfection of a lower and simpler species as such. Surely the songs of Schubert, Schumann, Mendelssohn, and Franz, or the symphonies by which the three former composers and Liszt have enriched our literature, cannot leave any doubt about the vitality of these forms, founded as they are on Beethoven's reformatory idea, and bearing witness to the high aspirations of their authors.

3.

We have completed the first part of our task; the reader who has followed us patiently in the course of our investigations will, we hope, have a distinct idea of the key-note of a movement which hitherto he was satisfied to know by the vague name of the Music of the Future. He will understand what we, the believers in this future and its art, are struggling for, what are our hopes and fears, what our ideals. It will now be my further duty to show, how far and in what way these hopes and aspirations are realised in the creations of Richard Wagner; for by a rare gift of nature he is endowed with the combined genius of music and poetry, and in him at last we must recognise the reformer who re-unites in the music-drama the two arts of poetry and music, which seemed to be separated by a profound chasm and in reality are one.

But before we enter into a new field of speculative inquiry, the reader will naturally feel anxious to be slightly introduced to the personality of the man, about whose achievements he has been hearing so much. The present writer is the more willing to meet this justifiable craving of the mind for the more solid nourishment of facts, after so much unsubstantial theory, as it appears to him that the cloud of dust raised by enemies and friends in their contest about the music of the future has enveloped Wagner himself in a mysterious atmosphere of contradictory rumours. I have repeatedly found serious difficulties in persuading English friends, particularly of the youthfully enthusiastic type, that our master is not quite a beginner just about to sow his wild oats in works like 'Tristan and Iseult' or the 'Rhinegold.' The most valuable material for the following dates has been taken from two autobiographical sketches written by Wagner at different periods of his career. The first contains a short account of his adventures up to 1842; the second is dated ten years later, and gives a most interesting survey of the master's youthful errors and longings, and their bearing upon the artistic deeds of his riper age. Both have been reprinted in the first and fourth volumes of his collected works. Other facts have been gleaned from biographical notices published at various times in newspapers and periodicals.

William Richard Wagner was born at Leipsic on May 22nd, 1813. His father occupied a post in the municipal government of that city, and was trusted with the management of the town police by Maréchal Davoust during the French occupation, he, it is said, being the only one amongst his colleagues, who was able to converse fluently with the conquerors in their own language. He died soon after the liberation of the German territory, and left a family of seven children, of whom the last-born, our composer, was still in his earliest infancy. The widow's second husband was Ludwig Geyer, a portrait painter, who had formerly been an actor, and retained his interest in dramatic poetry to the end of his life. This circumstance seems to be the only connecting link between Wagner's family and the stage, which was to become of such decisive importance not only to his own artistic career, but also to those of his brothers and sisters. They almost all temporarily belonged to the theatrical profession, and Wagner's eldest brother again bequeathed his talent to his two daughters, one of whom, Johanna, acquired a high reputation as a singer and actress. She took the part of Elizabeth at the first performance of her uncle's opera *Tannhäuser*. Only our master himself entertained from the beginning a strong aversion against appearing as an actor in public; he himself ascribes his idiosyncrasy against the paraphernalia of the modern stage to the deep impression which the severe grandeur of the antique drama produced on his youthful mind. His strong imitative tendency, by which the first awakening of genius may generally be recognised, might have led him to his stepfather's second profession, but the early loss of the kind man soon removed this passing inclination from the boy's mind; moreover, he had been found an awkward pupil in his few attempts at handling charcoal and pencil.

In the chief representative of poetry in music, it cannot astonish us to see, that his first aspirations were entirely of the poetic kind, and that only through these he was led to the complementary aid of musical expression. The first flights of his youthful muse we have to date back as far as 1826, when we encounter Wagner as a not very industrious or hopeful pupil of the Kreuzschule, at Dresden, age thirteen. He had been studying English in order to understand Shakespeare, and the overpowering impression of his works was responsible for the first outbreak of Wagner's juvenile eccentricity. The result was an enormous tragedy, a kind of compound of 'Hamlet' and 'King Lear.' The following is Wagner's own humorous description of his monstrous first-born: "I had murdered forty-two people in the course of my piece, and was obliged to let most of them reappear as ghosts in the last acts for want of living characters." It was not long afterwards, at Leipsic, where the family had removed, that Wagner became acquainted with the great works of Beethoven, whose death about the same time passed not without a deep impression on the young enthusiast. The music to Goethe's 'Egmont' by this master excited his admiration to such a degree that he at once saw the necessity of a similar musical accompaniment to his own tragedy, and, notwithstanding his ignorance of counterpoint and thorough-bass, boldly decided to supply the want from his own resources. This led to a rapid perusal of some theoretical works, and in its further consequences to Wagner's adoption of the musical profession. Childish and grotesque though these ebullitions of precocious conceit may appear, we cannot but discover with hopeful joy, and accept as a good omen, the two names of Shakespeare and Beethoven at the outset of our master's thorny way to the pure heights of self-conscious artistic purpose.

As a third decisive element in Wagner's early self-education, we may add the history and mythology of antique Greece. This, in preference to the more accessible knowledge of Latin, he studied with an ardour, which proved extinguishable only by the pedantic drill of his schoolmasters at Leipsic. But the all-engrossing longing for artistic utterance soon expelled all minor interests from our master's soul. He began to neglect his philological studies completely, without, however, supplying them by seriously entering into the theoretical foundation of his chosen art. As yet the Titanic impetuosity of his nature shunned the limits of artistic measure, and was prone to see in every rule a fetter. He began treating various dramatic subjects, after his own fashion, producing verses and music simultaneously, without any settled plan as to the general course of the action. An overture composed about this period, which he himself calls the "climax of his nonsensicalities," was played at the Leipsic Theatre, but excited only irrepressible merriment on the part of the audience. But with undaunted energy he turned to other plans, the firm belief in his own vocation being the only guiding star on his sea of dark, indefinable longings. His theoretical knowledge of music was all this time utterly neglected. The *technique* of the piano he disdained to acquire, looking down upon that supplementary instrument with a contempt characteristic of the future master of instrumentation. But even the intricacies of harmony were at that period unravelled by him. With the sole exception of a course of contrapuntal studies, under the excellent Cantor Weinlig, he, indeed, never underwent much regular musical training. He himself acknowledges this absence of a systematic education, and ascribes to it greatly his indomitable energy in following untrodden paths, or, as he symbolically calls it, the fatal gift of "the never contented spirit which always seeks the new." But this spirit soon led him to the only true source of self-purification, which he found in the works of the great masters of his art, and most of all in the sublime efforts of Beethoven's genius. The following extract from Schumann's musical paper of 1838, may illustrate the zealous earnestness, which at that time already was characteristic of all Wagner's doings. It was written by Heinrich Dorn, then a friend, and now a fierce adversary of our master. "I am doubtful," he says, "whether there ever has been a young musician more familiar with the works of Beethoven, than Wagner was at eighteen. He possessed most of the master's overtures, and large instrumental scores in copies made by himself; he went to bed with the sonatas, and rose again with the quartetts. He sang the songs and whistled the concerti, for with the playing he could not get on very well; in brief there was in him a regular *furor Teutonicus*, which, combined with considerable scientific culture, and a peculiar activity of the mind, promised powerful shoots."

At the time to which the date of this sketch takes us, Wagner was the conductor of a second-rate opera at Riga, a position which, unsatisfactory as it was, must still be considered as an improvement upon similar employments held by him before in middle-sized cities of North Germany.

The intervening period we might call the prehistoric time which we notice in the artistic careers of many great musicians. What has become of all the Italian operas which Handel and Mozart composed to order and by the dozen? Their titles are dimly discernible to the student of musical history, and one may occasionally meet with an air selected from them in the concert-hall or the drawing-room; otherwise they have dwindled again into oblivion and nothingness. Nearly the same applies to the various productions of Wagner's early years. We will not encumber the memory of the reader with the analysis of a symphony, several overtures, and other miscellaneous compositions, nor with the names of various operas, which would have to remain names only. One of the latter, the subject of which was taken from Shakespeare's 'Measure for Measure,' was performed once at Magdeburg without due preparation or marked success. This work is considered by its author as the ultimate result of the sensual fermentation of his storm and stress period, but not without a germ of purer artistic aims.

The personal history of our artist during this interval contains only a few remarkable incidents. It presents the usual mixture of extravagant schemes, remorseful disappointment and misery, in which so many hopes and gifts have perished. The pressing anxieties of his affairs were still increased by his marriage with an actress at Königsberg, in whom, however, he was not to find a congenial sympathiser with his artistic interests, nor even a careful helpmate in the troubles of daily life. His position in Riga marked, as we have seen, a slight advance in his prospects, but still was not of the kind to satisfy the demands of Wagner's energy for a wider sphere of action. It belonged to the duties of his office to conduct the silliest productions of the French and Italian stages. There is something inexpressibly tragic in the idea of his rehearsing with the mediocre band and singers of a provincial theatre, the trivial pieces of Adam and Donizetti. Still Wagner tried to make the best of the means at his disposal. We have the testimony of the theatrical manager at Riga, that he never had a conductor who did his duty more conscientiously and willingly than our master, the only drawback being that the players and singers strongly objected to the careful study and intelligent rendering of their parts, expected from them, quite against the usual lackadaisical habits of the stage. This hard apprenticeship may have contributed a great deal to secure to Wagner in later years that unequalled firmness and presence of mind, which now entitles him to the universally acknowledged leadership amongst living conductors.*

Another valuable experience of this time was Wagner's acquaintance with the strong dramatic lights and shades, as they are interwoven with the trivial sentimentalities of the average Italian opera; traces of the skilful handling so acquired can be recognised throughout his works, and distinguish them favourably from the awkward clumsiness of most German dramatists. But, nevertheless, the giant

* See Appendix I.

found his situation amongst a set of uncongenial, nay even inimical, pygmies more and more intolerable; he resolved to break his fetters, and in true giant fashion he began by attempting impossibilities. It struck him that Paris would be the right place to realise his dreams of happiness and glory, and who could be a better man to introduce his works to the capital of the world than Scribe, the celebrated *librettiste* of Meyerbeer and other stars of the grand opera? To Scribe, therefore, he sends the scheme of a great dramatic work, asking him to write it in French verse at the expense of the composer, and at the same time to take preliminary steps for its performance at the opera. The result of this cavalier offer from an utterly unknown composer, without even an introduction, was as might be expected,—no answer.

But this first failure was not able to damp Wagner's enthusiasm. If Scribe refuses to write him a text, he is quite the man to supply himself with one. His choice of a subject fell on Bulwer's novel, 'Rienzi;' and after having finished the whole poem and the music to the first two acts, he embarked with his wife on board a sailing vessel, which was to take him to London, *en route* for

Paris. The voyage was long and unfavourable; they were driven out of their course, and once during a storm the captain had to seek shelter in a Norwegian port. After nearly a month they reached at last their destination, remained a short time in London, and continued their journey. In the autumn of 1839, Wagner arrived at Paris with introductions from Meyerbeer to theatrical managers and full of hopes of seeing his work performed. We almost shudder in thinking of the fatal consequences which a great success might have had on Wagner's creative power. Perhaps he would have been content with the doubtful honour of sharing with Meyerbeer the lucrative laurels of a European reputation. Luckily for himself and his art, Fortune handled him with all the relentless cruelty which she seems to reserve especially for the children of genius. His visit to Paris proved an utter failure. All his attempts at testing the vitality of his work by the ordeal of a performance before the critical French audience were in vain. In order to earn a scanty livelihood, he had to undergo the most humiliating trials of musical drudgery; and even in this way he narrowly escaped the death from starvation which he described with

grim humour in his novelette: 'The End of a
Musician in Paris.' We may consider it as the
most irrefutable test of Wagner's real genius
that he did not perish in this overpowering sea
of misery and sorrow. It was the original longing of his nature for the purer aims of art that
broke into the night of his despair, and taught
him now, when every hope of worldly success
had vanished, to seek refuge in the joys of spontaneous creation, which is regardless of ephemeral
applause. The instinct of the true artist led
him to the inexhaustible source of popular imagination, as the only congenial companion of his
ideal art, and his searching eye soon discovered two
mythological types, as the poetical representatives
of his own sufferings and aspirations. They were
the *Flying Dutchman*, homeless and longing for
home, on the pitiless waves of a borderless ocean;
and *Tannhäuser*, satiated with the bitter pangs of
pleasure, and released from the thraldom of lust by
the responsive love of pure womanhood. The
genesis of the first mentioned libretto is of
peculiar interest to the English reader, as its
origin in Wagner's version seems indirectly connected with this country, and deserves a particular

mentioning as one of the few benefits which the master owes to England. The following is a *résumé* of my researches in this direction :—

The story of the *Flying Dutchman* can be traced back as far as the sixteenth century, and like that of his fellow-sufferer by land, the Wandering Jew, seems to be an outgrowth of the thoroughly revolutionised and exalted state of feeling caused by the two great events of those times—the discovery of a new world by the Spaniards, and of a new faith by the Germans. Captain Vanderdecken, as is generally known, tries to double the Cape of Good Hope notwithstanding a heavy gale blowing dead in his teeth, and finding this task too much for him, the obstinate Dutchman swears that he will carry out his purpose, even if he should have to sail till doomsday. The Evil One, hearing this oath, accepts it in its most literal meaning, and in consequence the unfortunate sailor is doomed to roam for ever and aye on the ocean, far from his wife and his beloved Holland. However, the poets of later ages, pitying the weary wanderer of the main, have tried in different ways to release him from this desolate fate. Captain Marryat in his well-known novel has not been very fortunate in this respect. Another *dénouement* of the story was invented by Heinrich Heine, and upon this Wagner has avowedly based the poem of his opera. In Heine's fragmentary story, 'The Memoirs of Herr von Schnabelewopski,' the hero (who, by the bye, shows only slightly disguised the characteristic features of the great humorist himself) tells us how on his passage from Hamburg to Amsterdam he saw a vessel with blood-red sails, very likely the phantom ship of the Flying Dutchman, whom shortly afterwards he beheld *in ipsissima persona* on the stage of the last-named city. The new feature added to the old story is this:—that, instead of an unconditional sentence, Vanderdecken is condemned to wander till doomsday, *unless* he shall have been released by the love of a woman "faithful unto death." The Devil (stupid as he is) does not believe in the virtue of women, and therefore allows the unhappy captain to go ashore once every seven years, in order to take a wife. The poor Dutchman has been disappointed in his attempts at finding such a paragon of faithful spouses for many a time, till at last, just after another period of seven years has elapsed, he meets a Scotch (according to Wagner, a Norwegian) merchant, and readily obtains his paternal consent to a proposed marriage with his daughter. This daughter herself has formed a romantic attachment for the unfortunate sailor, whose story she has heard and whose picture hangs in her room. When she sees the real Flying Dutchman she recognises him at once by the resemblance with his likeness, and, heroically deciding to share his fate, accepts the offer of his hand. At this moment Schnabelewopski-Heine is (by an unforeseen and indescribable incident) called away from the house, and, when he comes back, is just in time to see the Dutchman on board his own ship, which is weighing anchor for another voyage of hopeless despair. He loves his bride, and would save her from the fate that threatens her if she accompanies him. But she, "faithful unto death," ascends a high rock and throws herself into the waves, by which heroic deed the spell is broken, and the Flying Dutchman, united with his bride, enters the long closed gates of eternal rest.

Heine pretends, as we have said, to have seen this acted on the Amsterdam stage; this statement, however, he withdrew afterwards, and emphatically claimed as his own the invention of the beautiful and eminently dramatic episode. The former statement was also in so far inaccurate that he never sailed from Hamburg to Holland; his voyage was, on the contrary, directed to London, and here most likely it was also that he made the acquaintance of the *Flying Dutchman* in a theatrical capacity. The story of the Phantom Ship seems to have been at that time (1827) to a certain extent popular in England. A very impressive version of it had appeared in 'Blackwood's Magazine' (May, 1821), and this was made the groundwork of a melodramatic production of the late Mr. Fitzball, a playwright of those days, whose adaptations were as numerous and quite as "original" as those of some contemporary stage favourites. The piece in question is extremely silly and bad in every respect. Mynheer Vanderdecken here is the slave and ally of some horrid monster of the deep, and his motive in taking a wife is only to increase the number of his victims. In this wicked purpose, however, he does not succeed—the heroine escaping his snares and marrying (if I remember rightly) a young officer whom she had loved against the will of her father. This piece was running at the Adelphi Theatre about the time of Heine's visit to London;

and nothing is more probable than that the German poet, who conscientiously studied the English stage, should have seen it. For the circumstance of the Dutchman's taking a wife, Heine would in that case be indebted to Fitzball, in whose piece there also occurs an old picture connected with the story. It would thus be most interesting to note, how Heine developed out of these trivial indications his noble idea of the Dutchman's deliverance by the love of a woman. Wagner, on his part, has heightened the dramatic pathos of the fable by making his hero symbolise a profound philosophical idea—thus raising the conception of his character from the sphere of a popular tale into that of artistic significance, out of fancy into imagination. The pitiful figure of Mynheer Vanderdecken becomes an embodiment of life-weariness, longing for death, and forgetfulness of individual pain and struggle, or (which is the same) of existence.

Still, we must acknowledge, it would seem, that the modest germs of these grand ideas were furnished to both the German poet and composer by the English playwright; and we must further note that it was on a voyage to the British shores that both the one and the other conceived the scheme of their work. For I need not tell the reader, who may have witnessed a performance of the *Flying Dutchman* at Drury Lane, that the wild atmosphere of seas and storms hovering over the whole piece is the reflex of Wagner's own impressions during his eventful passage from Riga to London. The piece was finished two years later, in only seven weeks, when Wagner had left Paris for a short stay in the country. After an interruption of his creative labours for nearly nine months, Wagner felt himself a musician again, and this consciousness of a higher task restored him courage and strength in the renewed battle of life.

The contrast between the spectacular effects (combined though they may appear with great dramatic power) in *Rienzi*, and the purely artistic means of rendering emotional accents, aimed at in the *Dutchman*, is at once striking and relieving. It resembles the sense of freedom one feels in passing from the scented atmosphere of a crowded operahouse into the bracing air of sea and forest.

But it is in a still higher sense that the latter work signifies the ideal regeneration, the antique "Katharsis" of Wagner as a man and artist. Up to this time brilliant success had been the chief aim of his thoughts; now that disappointment and misery had weaned the strong man from his cherished hopes, he retired into himself, intent upon following the call of his only remaining friend, the true muse. The *Flying Dutchman* was begun without a hope, almost without a wish, for outward success; he only felt that what he had to say was true to himself, and so he said it, listen who liked. In this way, and urged only by the necessity of his nature, Wagner entered upon his new career without imagining himself the bearing of his reformatory act on the progress of art in general.

In the meanwhile his affairs had taken a more favourable turn. Quite against his expectation, *Rienzi* had been accepted by the Court Theatre at Dresden, with the additional flattering invitation to the master to conduct his work himself. In the spring of 1842 he returned to Germany, and crossed the Rhine with the tears of joy and renewed home-feeling in his eyes. He also visited the Castle of Wartburg, the scene of his projected *Tannhäuser*, on his way to Dresden. In October, 1842, *Rienzi* was performed for the first time, and the brilliant success of the work led to

Wagner's engagement as conductor of the Royal Opera. The unexpected change in his condition, from a friendless stranger in a foreign land to the leader of one of the greatest art institutions in his own country, could not but fill our master with joyful surprise. But the dream of happiness was of short duration. Notwithstanding the unusual success of *Rienzi* at Dresden, the great German theatres showed little inclination to open their gates to the new-comer; and even where his works were accepted, the public were at first more taken by surprise than pleased at the unusual force of this new language. The bitter disappointment felt by Wagner at the first performances of his *Dutchman* at Berlin, and of *Tannhäuser* at Dresden, could not but convince him—particularly if he remembered the storms of applause excited by his spectacular first-born—that what he wished to say could as yet be directed only to a few sympathising friends.

This sense of isolation, combined with his daily experience of the utter want of artistic aims and principles in the management of the great German theatres, surrounded him with an atmosphere of morbid discontentedness in which a change at any price seemed a relief, and it was in this mood that he, although little of a politician, joined the insurrectionary movement of 1848, and 1849 by word and deed. Two pamphlets written during this period prove how, even in the highest excitement of active partisanship, he never lost sight of his artistic mission. One of them relates to the foundation of a truly national theatre at Dresden, while the other, 'Art and Revolution,' tries to demonstrate the close connection between the regeneration of political life and similar tendencies in contemporary art.

The Titan was again progressing in enormous strides towards Utopia. But, alas for the clumsy realities of our earthly existence! The revolution at Dresden was crushed by Prussian bayonets, and Wagner had once more to take up his staff and fly the country as an exile. After a short sojourn at Paris, where he seemed to be drawn by a sort of unacknowledged fascination, and where with equal certainty bitterest disappointment lay in wait for him, he retired to Switzerland, severed from his friends and country, and without the shadow of a hope of ever being able again to interpret his works to his nation.

This weight of misery would have crushed a

weaker man; Wagner's dramatic nature rose up in the contest, riding on the billows that were to submerge him. The conductor's baton was wrenched from his hand, so he took up the pen of the critic, attacking in their turn and without distinction or mercy all classes of society, musical conductors and authors, critics, Jews, and actresses, but most of all those mercenaries in his own branch of art who, making " a milch cow of the divine goddess," overflowed the stage with the shallow display of their commonplace artificialities. The mere invention of the incomparable term 'Kapellmeistermusik' for this kind of production would secure Wagner a prominent place amongst satirical writers.

That the goad of his invective was always wisely directed and used with discretion we should be sorry to assert. But it must be remembered that in cleansing the stables of Augias, one cannot be expected to be over nice in his distinctions; moreover, the combative side of Wagner's power, which prevents him from discerning the pure gold in a mass of alloy, is too closely interwoven with the whole bias of his nature not to be gladly accepted by his friends. The bird's-eye view from the sublime heights of genius must needs ignore many of those minute differences and considerations with which we mortals of smaller stature are obliged to reckon. Besides, a great man must be accepted or renounced as a whole, like the sea or the sun in heaven. If you look at it through the lens of a dissecting criticism, its splendour will be diffused in single rays of moderate lighting power; so the demigod will look very much like an ordinary mortal, not because he has ceased to be the *hero*, but because you are the *valet* of the proverb.

And, after all, the polemical part forms only a small and comparatively unimportant fraction of Wagner's writings. It was by means of these theoretical speculations that he himself for the first time became conscious of the enormous bearing of his own artistic deeds on the progress of music. What he had done hitherto was more like a groping in the dark for the dazzling splendour of a distant light, than the steady progress of the accomplished artist in the bright rays of his ideal aspirations. Not that his later works are any the less the immediate creations of impulse. On the contrary, we hear in them more and more distinctly the sound of the unfettered wings of purest inspiration. Only the level from which these inspired wings now start on their sunward flight is higher, and therefore the atmosphere in which they move purer than before, or, to speak without metaphor, through the processes of metaphysical thought and historical study Wagner had become conscious of the ultimate aims of his and of all art, and also of the legitimate means by which this aim might be attained. Fortified by this knowledge against the temptations of ephemeral success, he was able once more to surrender his nature unconditionally to the free impulse of his genius. In the works of his later period, like *Tristan* and the *Meistersinger*, the traces of uncertainty in the handling of the artistic material, or, still worse, of mere theatrical effects which occasionally mar the highest beauties in *Tannhäuser* and *Lohengrin*, have entirely disappeared. We now distinguish, in the pure proportions of the whole as well as in the finish of the minutest details, the hand of the master, in the full consciousness of his reformatory mission.

The chief features of this reform, as marked in the later works of Wagner, we must now consider a little more closely.

4.

In order to appreciate fully the position of Wagner's dramas in the development of music, we have to distinguish two different sides of their import. First of all we recognise in them an energetic protest against the established artificialities of a demoralised operatic stage. We have seen before how the opera itself, based as it was on a misunderstood imitation of the antique drama, had in the course of time completely lost what little there might have been of dramatic economy in its original structure. In Italy the predominant importance of musical forms had entirely disarranged the harmonious proportions of the opera, while, in the latest phase of the lyric stage in France, the morbid craving for spectacular effects of the lower order exceeded all bounds of nature and common sense, not to speak of the elevated principles of art. But even men of pure intentions and high genius were not able to embody their inspirations in a form of art the organism of which was diseased to the core, and in which the principles of music and poetry were so strangely at variance, that, instead of a desirable mutual assistance, they could not but continually check and chain each other's movements.

All this was thoroughly changed by Wagner. He has crushed the hard fetters of petrified formalities in the firm grasp of his hand, remoulding the dead metal by the burning breath of his genius into new shapes of harmonious fashion. His operas are no longer a series of separate pieces of music, like duets, arias, and finales, with little reference to the action of the piece, and loosely connected with each other by the weak thread of dry recitativi. His last and supreme purpose is the attainment of dramatic truth ; and from this point of view we must consider the process of condensation and self-restraint to which Wagner ultimately sacrificed the whole apparatus of absolute musical forms. The first and most dangerous excrescence of the opera which he attacked was the aria. This musical equivalent of the monologue of the spoken drama had, in the course of time, obtained an undue importance. It was considered by both the composer and the singer as a welcome test of their musical capacities, and had, in consequence, to be inserted into the piece without rhyme or reason, wherever those two omnipotent rulers of the unfortuate *librettiste* thought fit.

Wagner has totally abolished the aria proper.

The whole weight of his musical energy is placed into the dialogue as the chief factor of the action, and is fashioned entirely according to the requirements of this action, rising with it where an occasion offers into the intensest fervour of lyrical exaltation, and always surrounding it with a flow of beautiful melody, but without ever misleading its course into the dangerous channels of ill-applied sentimentality. It need not be added that also the other forms of absolute music, like ensemble and finale, etc., were swept away by the force of this dramatic energy, but Wagner (and in this we have to recognise the *positive* and reconstructive side of his revolution) has at the same time created a new form of musical expression, which originates from, and varies with the impulse of dramatic passion; nay, which is nothing but this passion intensified and idealised by the divinest of arts; the *logos*, which has shaken off its earthly raiments and is transferred once more to its own ethereal sphere.

The definite appearance of this new mode of expression it would be impossible to describe without an endless number of musical quotations. And even with those the *reader* would be unable to realise the feeling of harmonious enjoyment with which the perfect unity and appropriateness of these forms affects the *hearer*.

I will mention only one point which bears equally on the poetical and the musical side of the question, and is, therefore, not so entirely withdrawn from an explanation, as where the latter art alone is concerned.

We have seen how Wagner's musical inspiration flows entirely from the conditions of his dramatic subject. It was only natural that even for the rhythmical structure of his *melos*, he should look to its poetical foundation. Modern verse could offer him but little assistance in this respect. In it metrical arsis and thesis, as they existed in antique poetry have been entirely supplanted by the rhetorical accent of the words; and the different forms of verse founded on this principle prove often rather an impediment than an aid to musical composition. The important attraction of rhyme is, for example, entirely useless to the musician; blank verse, on the other hand, is a most unwieldy combination for musical purposes, and can indeed only be treated like prose.

In this difficulty Wagner looked for help to the metrical basis of all Teutonic poetry, *i.e.* the alliterative principle or *staffrhyme*, as he found it in the 'Edda' and other remnants of ancestral lore. His last great work, the subject of which is also taken from the old sagas, is written in a modified reproduction of the old metre which Wagner treats with eminent skill, and very much in the same manner as Mr. Morris and Mr. E. Magnusson have done in our language in their admirable translations from the Icelandic.*

The gain of this new method for Wagner's music is inestimable. The strong accents of the alliterating syllables supply his melody with rhythmical firmness; while, on the other hand, the unlimited number of low-toned syllables allow full liberty to the most varied *nuances* of declamatory expression. In order to exemplify the step in advance, I will ask the reader to compare the song of Wolfram in *Tannhäuser* ('Dir hohe Liebe'), where the iambic metre has been obliterated and the verse constantly cut to pieces by the musical cæsura, with the wonderful love song from the *Valkyre* ('Winterstürme wichen'), where verse and

* The story of the 'Volsungs and Nibelungs.' Translated from the Icelandic by E. Magnusson and William Morris. London. Ellis.

melody seem to glide on together in harmonious rhythms like the soft winds of spring of which they tell.

Our last remarks have shown us our composer in the new light of a poet. The reader is probably aware of the fact that Wagner, from his first opera to his last, supplied himself with the words to his music; and the advance which we have pointed out in the latter art, we can trace in commensurate degrees in his dramatic writings.

The text of *Rienzi* displays a good deal of that slovenliness in diction and versification, which the good-natured public of the grand opera is used to tolerate. But when in the *Flying Dutchman*, Wagner left the spectacular effects of the so-called "historical" school for the popular myth, as the unalloyed source of the purely human, his style at once rose with the greater requirements of his task. The fettering chrysalis was slipped off and the beautiful butterfly raised it wings; the *librettiste* had become a *poet*.

Wagner himself has given us the cue to the hidden causes of this transition, which at the same time affords new evidence of the strict reciprocity of his musical and poetical faculties. "In *Rienzi*," he says, "my only purpose was to write an opera, and thinking only of this opera, I took my subject as I found it ready made in another man's finished production. . . . . With the *Flying Dutchman*, I entered upon a new course, by becoming the artistic interpreter of a subject which was given to me only in the simple crude form of a popular tale.* From this time I became, with regard to all my dramatic works, first of all a *poet;* and only in the ultimate completion of the poem my faculty as a *musician* was restored to me. But as a poet I was again from the beginning conscious of my power of expressing musically the import of my subjects. This power I had exercised to such a degree, that I was perfectly certain of my ability of applying it to the realisation of my poetical purpose, and therefore, was at much greater liberty to form my dramatic schemes according to their poetical necessities, than if I had conceived them from the beginning with a view to their musical treatment. . . . . What we want to express in

---

* In comparing this statement with what we have said about Heine's treatment of the 'Flying Dutchman' legend, the reader ought to remember that this treatment comprises only the merest outline of the story, and purposely retains the tone of its popular origin.

music are only feelings and sensations; music renders in its fullest sway the pure emotional foundation of the word which in our essentially logical speech cannot be severed from its mixture of reasoning; it is only the power of expressing distinctly the separate and individual, that music gains by its blending with worded utterance. If this connection is to be fruitful, there must be in the words themselves an innate want and desire for pure sentimental expression, and by this the nature of the musico-poetical speech itself is sufficiently defined. It can be nothing but the purely human, freed from the fetters of all conventionalities."

It was in this way that Wagner, by the requirements of his musical genius, was led from the formal relations of historical characters to the unimpeded freedom of mythical types. But this progress at the same time implied reactively the liberation of this music itself from the arbitrary limits of tradition. It is true that in the choice and treatment of his subjects, Wagner was unconsciously guided by his musical instinct, but between this and the adoption of the abstract forms of music there was a vast difference.

"The plastic unity and simplicity," he continues,

"of the mythical subject-matter allowed of the concentration of the action on certain important and decisive points of its development; thus I was enabled to rest on those fewer scenes with a perseverance sufficient to expound the subject down to its last dramatic consequences. The nature of the subject could, therefore, not induce me, in sketching my scenes to consider in advance their adaptability to any abstract musical form, the particular kind of musical treatment being necessitated by these scenes themselves. It could not enter my mind to ingraft on this *my* musical form, growing as it did out of the nature of the scenes, the traditional forms of operatic music, which could only have marred and interrupted its organic progress. I, therefore, never thought of contemplating, on principle and as a deliberate reformer, the destruction of the aria, the duet, and other operatic forms; but the dropping of these forms followed consistently from the nature of my subjects." With this we have nearly finished our sketch of the most important features of Wagner's music-drama, or, as it has also been called, The Work of Art of the Future. Other characteristics we shall occasionally mention in the further course of our remarks. Only to one more point I would fain call the reader's attention, as it has given rise to a great deal of discussion, and forms an important item amongst the heads of impeachment, raised by our master's adversaries against him.

In his 'Oper und Drama,' Wagner urges the demand of a co-operation of all the arts, that is, of painting and architecture as well as of poetry and music, in the drama of the future. It, therefore, cannot surprise us to see that in his own attempts at realising this ideal work of art, considerable importance has been placed on the visible beauties of the action, as far as they may be attained by the painting of scenery and the grouping of human figures.

Wagner's stage directions are always of the minutest, and show all that skill and knowledge of scenic effects which so favourably distinguishes him from most other German dramatists. But the honest Teuton critics stand amazed at this unwonted display of taste and elegance in the highest sense, which to them savours of French *raffinement* and other dangerous and evil things. They summarily condemn the dazzling splendour of scenery as unworthy of the simplicity of fatherlandish manners and tastes. In order to prove the futility of such overstrained purism let us just consider the first occurring case in point. In the first act of *Tannhäuser*, when the knight, satiated by the overmeasure of joy in the realm of love's goddess, resolves to leave her, he invokes against the bewitching charms of Venus the idea of the Mother of God as the prototype of love in its purest emanation. The moment he utters the name of 'Mary,' the spell is broken, the 'Venusberg' sinks into the abyss, and we involuntarily draw a deep breath as we emerge from its close-scented atmposhere into the fresh air of a beautiful spring landscape, full of sun and flowers, and made musical with the song of a lonely shepherd. The effect of this sudden change is indescribable and of the purest poetic kind, although entirely achieved by means of a shifted piece of pasteboard.

And the same may be said of all the scenic effects in Wagner's operas. They are made throughout subservient to the economy of the drama, with the organism of which they are connected as closely as music and poetry themselves. To compare this legitimate use of the appliances of the modern stage with the interruption of the action by melodramatic *spectacle*, as we see it, for instance, in the celebrated burning vessel of Meyerbeer's still more celebrated *Africaine*, is an absurdity which requires no further refutation.

5.

We should now have to return to the personal career of our master, whom we left in his retirement in Switzerland, but that the facts which relate to his reappearance on the public stage as a composer and conductor after a seclusion of nearly ten years, are so recent, and so closely connected with the fates and sympathies of other living persons, that a calm historical account would become almost impossible. I must, therefore, limit myself here to a chronological survey of his works, which in his, as in most cases, seem to be the best if not only *rapport* between the living master and his public.

We have in our former observations described the genesis of Wagner's two acknowledged first operas, *Rienzi* and the *Flying Dutchman*. It has also been mentioned how, during his stay at Paris already, he was deeply impressed with the beauties of the popular story of 'Tannhäuser,' the knight and singer, whose sin and repentance Wagner has since surrounded with the aureole of his genius. The composition of this work was finished during the winter 1844-45.

The next subject to which he turned, was in form and idea the very counterpart of the tragic elevation of the last-mentioned opera. It transfers us from the romantic surroundings of the mediæval castle of Wartburg into the domestic narrowness of a worthy artisan's household during the sixteenth century. The 'Mastersingers of Nürnberg,' with their homely conception of life and art, were intended by Wagner originally as a kind of humorous pendant to the knightly poets in 'Tannhäuser,' from which however the redeeming features of true honesty and justified self-assertion were not absent. The character of 'Hans Sachs,' in its present conception as the type of the rising importance of middle-class freedom and intelligence towards the close of the mediæval period, is one of Wagner's finest creations. However, this attempt at a modified revival of the antique satyr-drama was for the time abandoned in favour of another romantic subject, viz., 'Lohengrin,' the Knight of the Swan. I shall take a later opportunity of giving a close analysis of this beautiful and important work, and will add here only that, compared with 'Tannhäuser,' it marks a further stage in its author's progress towards the ultimate aim of pure dramatic expression. It was finished in March, 1848, but was not performed till two years later at Weimar, when the energetic action of Franz Liszt once more rallied the friends of the banished master round the standard of the Future.

During the musical composition of *Lohengrin*, the old contest in Wagner's mind between the historical and mythical principles was also finally decided. The representative of the former was Siegfried, the hero of the oldest manifestations of Teutonic religious feeling; that of the latter, Frederic the First, the great Emperor of the Hohenstaufen dynasty, whose return from his sleep of centuries was, till quite lately, connected by the German people with the revival of the old imperial glory. I need not add that the victory remained with Siegfried. Wagner began at once sketching the subject, but gradually the immense breadth and grandeur of the old types began to expand under his hands, and the result was a trilogy or rather tetralogy of enormous dimensions, perhaps the most colossal attempt upon which the dramatic muse has ventured since the times of Aeschylus.

The four dramatic poems which form the cyclus of the 'Ring of the Nibelung' were written as early as the middle of 1852, and the three next years were partly occupied in writing the music to the introductory drama, the 'Rhinegold,' and to the first part of the trilogy, the 'Valkyre.'

At this point the continuation of the vast scheme was interrupted by another work of no lesser grandeur and beauty of conception. It was this, the tragedy of 'Tristan and Iseult.' The poem was begun in 1856, and the music finished in 1859. The performance of the work was delayed by various circumstances till 1865, when it took place under Von Bülow's excellent direction at Munich. The enormous importance of 'Tristan and Iseult,' for the progress of modern music, was at once recognised by friends and enemies, who made its name the hue and cry in their fierce debate. This prominent position of the work may also be my excuse for reproducing here, with a few alterations, the remarks I made on its musical and poetical beauties, on the occasion of a selection from it being produced at a recent concert of the London Wagner Society. The passage of the programme referred to runs thus:—

TRISTAN AND ISOLDE.

INTRODUCTION AND CLOSE OF THIRD ACT - *Wagner.*

Tristan und Isolde is the fifth of Wagner's acknowledged dramatic works, its first performance (at Munich in 1865) following that of *Lohengrin* after an interval of fifteen years. The step in advance marked by it in its author's development, and in that of dramatic music in general, is proportionate to this lapse of time. According to his own assertion, Wagner wrote it with the full concentrated power of his inspiration, freed at last from the fetters of conventional operatic forms, with which he has broken here definitely and irrevocably. In *Tristan und Isolde* we hear for the first time the unimpaired language of dramatic passion, intensified by an uninterrupted flow of expressive melody, the stream of which is no longer obstructed or led into the artificial canals of aria, cavatina, etc. Here also the orchestra obtains that wide range of emotional expression which enables it, like the chorus of the antique tragedy, to discharge the dialogue of an overplus of lyrical elements, without weakening the intensity of the situation, which it accompanies like an unceasing passionate undercurrent.

It is also in *Tristan und Isolde* that we perceive most distinctly the powerful sway of Schopenhauer's philosophy, with its profound reproduction of the 'Nirwana' of individual existence, over our composer's mind. In our work the very passion of love is made the symbol of the supreme transfusion of the separate Ego into the nature of the beloved object.

After the stated facts, it cannot surprise us to see, that our music-drama (for Opera would be a decided misnomer) has become a bone of contention between the adherents of the liberal and conservative schools of music. Many people who greatly admire "certain things" in *Tannhäuser* and *Lohengrin* draw the line at *Tristan und Isolde*, which, on the other hand, is considered by the advanced party as the representative work of a new epoch in art. A musician's position to the present work may indeed be considered as the crucial test of his general tendency towards the past or future.

The subject of Wagner's tragedy is taken from the Celtic Mabinogi of *Tristrem and Iseult*, which at an early stage became popular amongst different nations, and found its most perfect mediæval treatment in Gottfried von Strassburg's immortal epic. Our modern poet has followed his original closely, pruning, however, and modifying where the economy of the drama seemed to require it. The episode of *Riwalin* and *Blancheflur*, and the early youth of *Tristan* remains unmentioned, and the scene opens on board the vessel, destined to carry the unwilling Irish bride to old *King Marke*. Despair and love's disappointment, together with the insult inflicted upon her family by *Tristan's* victory over her kinsman *Morolt*, rankle in *Isolde's* bosom, and drive her to the resolution of destroying her own life together with that of her beloved enemy. *Tristan* is invited to drink with her the cup of atonement, but, without *Isolde's* knowledge, the prepared poisonous draught is changed by her faithful companion *Brangaene* for the love philter. The reader will perceive at once the immense dramatic force of this version, compared with the old story, where the fatal potion is taken by a pure mistake. This potion itself becomes in Wagner only the symbol of irresistible love, which, to speak with the Psalmist, is "strong as death" and knows of no fetter.*

The further events of the drama are the consistent outgrowth of this tragic guilt. The second act contains the secret meeting of the lovers, which has given the composer occasion for a duet, the pathos and sweetness of which remain unequalled in dramatic literature. Betrayed by *Melot* (who from the mischievous dwarf of older versions has become a knight and *Tristan's* false friend) they are surprised by *King Marke*, and *Tristan*, crushed by the sad reproach of his benefactor, makes a feigned attack on *Melot*, who in return pierces his defenceless breast. In the third and last act *Tristan* is discovered lying in a state of unconsciousness at his castle in Brittany. His retainer, *Kurwenal*, has sent a messenger to *Isolde*, who once before has cured *Tristan* from the effects of a

* It ought to be mentioned that the same fine touch of treating the love potion as an entirely accidental matter, which occasions, but does not cause the affection between the ill-fated couple, is also found in the mediæval German poet.

terrible wound. *Tristan* awakes, and on being told of *Isolde's* approach, tears, in an ecstasy of joy, the bandage from his wound, which causes his death at the moment when his lost love comes to his rescue. *Isolde* expires on the body of her lover.

Our selection consists of the introduction to the drama, and the dying scene (Liebestod) of *Isolde*. The former piece is founded on one single motive of intensely passionate impressiveness, which is worked out thematically into various and, at the same time, concentrated shapes of great melodious beauty. The same melody forms a prominent feature of the music drama, and appears as "leading motive" wherever the composer wishes to suggest the idea of the love potion, or, as we have seen, of irresistible passion. To its strains also the names of *Tristan* and *Isolde* are uttered for the first time in fond whispering just after the fatal draught has been drained. We quote it here in full—

Langsam und schmachtend.

The dying scene of *Isolde* is conceived by the composer as a kind of sad echo of the happy union of the lovers in the second act. The principal motives of the latter scene reappear in the orchestral part as a fond remembrance of lost bliss, accompanied by the broken utterances of the voice. At the same time we have to recognise in this retrospective introduction of the same motives a symbolic expression of the lovers' reunion after death, quite as simple and significant as the intertwining rose and vine which grow on their graves in the old story.

On the opening motive, which displays the broad, deeply coloured melodiousness of Wagner in its full splendour, we might inscribe as motto Freiligrath's expression of "Ruhe in der Geliebten," *i. e.*, the becalmed contentment in love which follows after and again leads to the climax of passion. To illustrate its meaning more fully, we quote the verses which it is employed to illustrate in the second act:

   So starben wir, um ungetrennt,
   ewig einig ohne End,
   ohn' Erwachen ohn' Erbangen,
   namenlos in Lieb' umfangen,
   ganz uns selbst gegeben,
   der Liebe nur zu leben.

This motive is worked up into the following phrase, in which the double turn adds greatly to its sweet impressiveness, and is to be taken as an essential part of the melody, and not as a mere fioriture.

Our last motive, which also finishes the love scene in the second act, is expressive of the highest joy of united love, which, in the " Liebestod," the visionary trance of the dying *Isolde* recalls to her mind.

During the composition of *Tristan*, Wagner never lost sight of the great work of national poetry, which he henceforth considered as the chief task of his life. The music to the second part of the trilogy, 'Siegfried,' was begun in the autumn of 1856, and finished after many interruptions of various kinds in 1869. One of these interruptions consisted in the resumption of the scheme of the comic opera sketched by us in the foregoing pages. The rewriting of the text, and the composition of the music to the 'Mastersingers,' occupied him at intervals from the end of 1861 to 1867, in the October of which year the score was finished.

From that day to this the full energy of Wagner has been dedicated to the final completion, and the preparation for an eventual performance of his *Nibelungen*. It was natural that in the present condition of the German stage, with its motley programme of classic, romantic, French, German, Italian, serious, comic, and burlesque operas, a satisfactory representation of a work of this kind could not be expected. Neither the singer who had to act, nor the hearer who attended, at a performance of *La Favorita* on Tuesday, and was looking forward to Meyerbeer's *Africaine*— or, better still, to Offenbach's *Belle Hélène*—on the ensuing Sunday, were likely to raise their receptive faculties for the intervening days of the week to conceptions like those of 'Siegfried' and 'Brunhilde' in the *Dusk of the Gods*. Wagner, therefore, for a long time despaired of the visible realisation of his ideas, and strongly opposed the performances of separate parts of his work attempted at Munich. It was only a few years ago that the late celebrated pianist *Charles Tausig*, one of the master's most zealous adherents, in connection with a small number of his artistic friends, confidently decided upon appealing to the admirers of Wagner's art amongst his own and other nations for the necessary means of carrying out the composer's original idea, viz., to perform the *Nibelungen* at a theatre to be erected for the purpose, and by a select company in the manner of a great national festival, and before an audience, which in this way would be, like the artists themselves, entirely removed from the atmosphere of ordinary theatrical shows.

The national and artistic import of the work itself, combined with the irresistible sway which Wagner's genius began to evince more and more over the best amongst his nation, seemed to warrant the boldness of this design; and the appeal was, indeed, responded to with great enthusiasm, far beyond the limits of his own country.

Wagner societies were founded not only in the most important German cities, but also in Milan, Brussels, London, New York, etc.; and at the present moment the realisation of the scheme at

Bayreuth in the spring of 1875 seems no longer doubtful. The performance of the tetralogy will be prepared and conducted by Wagner himself, who in this way will be enabled to render the highest aspirations of his soul, called into life and made real in the ideal world of the drama.

It would, of course, be premature to judge about the artistic import and effect of a work like this, before it has been embodied in the shapes of the stage, for which it seems so eminently destined. I will consider it here from one, viz., the historical point of view; and this also only in so far as it marks in a manner the final result of our researches, the concluding link of that "circulus" which, as we have seen, is the symbol of progress in art as well as in all other human things. I am speaking of the strange analogy between Wagner's *Nibelungen* and the drama of the antique stage, which I perceive in the following three important points:—first, the relative position of poetry and music, the latter of which in both Wagner's and Sophocles' drama is strictly limited to receiving and idealising the intentions of the sister art, on which it never intrudes the conditions of its own separate existence.

A second point of resemblance seems to me to exist between the chorus of the antique and the orchestra of the modern tragedy, paradoxical as this may appear at first sight; for the orchestral part, which by Wagner has been raised from the secondary position of a mere accompaniment of the voices into an important factor of the dramatic organism, is enabled by his masterly treatment to render in its varied measures the lyrical and reflective elements of the action, resembling in this respect the antique chorus much more closely, than the hackneyed exclamations of combined joy or grief which the choral singers of the orthodox opera are wont to utter.

As the last and most important parallelism, we mention the mythical foundation, which in both dramas forms the ideal background of the individual action. From this Wagner himself expects the revival of modern art, and through it of national life in a manner too ideal, perhaps, to be ever realised in our actual existence, but which will always be counted amongst the most beautiful dreams of human genius. *Quod felix faustum fortunatumque sit.*

5

Here ends what it was my present purpose to say about the personal character and artistic deeds of a man, whose importance in the progress of music, whatever view one may take of it, is certainly of too deep a nature to be finally judged by contemporary criticism. I am myself but too conscious of the sketchy nature of my account, but cannot suppress at the same time a hope, that the reader may have recognised in my rough outline the features of a grand immortal countenance, wrought by nature's own hands, and stamped by her with the indelible sign of genius; a "hero" and "swallower of formulas" in the most emphatic sense Mr. Carlyle ever imparted to that word, but at the same time endowed with the gift of reconstructing what was eternal in the destroyed fabric, after a plan of his own form and fashion—a man, in short, whom you may love or hate intensely, but whom you must reckon with in one way or another, if not the book of artistic revelation shall be for ever sealed to you with seven seals.

It would be intruding too much upon the confidence of the reader if, after the many statements which had necessarily to remain unsupported by evidence in the foregoing pages, I did not fix upon a single specimen of our master's works in which the advance in music marked by his works could be shown in a more definite manner. For this purpose I have chosen his third music-drama, *Lohengrin*, a work particularly adapted in our case, as showing most of the important new features of Wagner's art, yet without some of the more striking anomalies of his latest productions, the beauty and necessity of which can be tested only by the immediate impression of a performance on the stage.

But, before entering upon this last and most pleasant part of our task, I think it will be necessary, by way of clearing our road, to say a few words about certain doubts and misunderstandings which I fear, even after my lengthy disquisitions, may arise in the reader's mind. This misgiving is corroborated by my own literary experience with regard to the case in point.

When, nearly two years ago, I published a paper on Wagner in the 'Fortnightly Review,' and in this way gave the first comprehensive account of the music of the future, which (as far as my knowledge goes) has appeared in the English language, the importance of the question at stake was at once recognised by the fact of several of our most influential journals raising their voices on the subject.* I am alluding in particular to a leading article in the 'Daily News,' which exhibited all the literary skill, but (if I may judge in my own case) not quite the more than common musical appreciation, by which that journal is so favourably distinguished. The popular prejudices of which the article made itself the mouthpiece may be summed up in the double assertion, that what I had designated as the fundamental idea of the "music of the future" was wanting in "any genuine novelty;" and, further, that if the poetical principle insisted upon were carried out, it would make all instrumental music impossible, and, moreover, lead in its ultimate consequences to the destruction of both arts.

It may be hoped that the attentive reader will be in a position to judge about these objections

* I am told, that some years ago an article on a similar subject appeared in the 'Westminster Review;' but as this seems to have passed comparatively unnoticed, I think I may, without presumption, lay claim to the honour of having for the first time drawn the attention of a wider circle of English readers to Wagner's creations.

according to their merits ; still, in order to go quite safe, I will insert my reply to the editor of the 'Daily News':

"It is far from my wish, to enter into any kind of controversy about the value of the 'music of the future' in general, or about the originality of what I think to be its fundamental idea. I know very well that what is generally called a 'new idea' is never invented by a single individual. Its compounds have been singly hovering in the air, as it were, felt and known by many, either in the form of a doctrine of the learned, or even in that of a popular truism. Still it remains the task of genius to develop its *disjecta membra* into an organic whole; and, if the idea is of an artistic kind, to prove its vitality by an act of creation. In this sense, and in this sense only, I claimed for Wagner the honour or dishonour (whichever it may be) of having urged theoretically, and shown by his creative productions, the necessity of a poetical basis of music. The meaning of the word 'poetical' in such combination, differs essentially from the sense in which the word is generally used, and this *nuance*, perhaps not sufficiently explained by me, has, I think, given rise to some misapprehension in your article. By 'poetical' I mean only the original passionate impulse, which every artist must feel, and which he tries to embody in his work, be it by means of articulate words, sounds, or colours. In this sense every artist must be first a poet; and without such a fundamental conception, poetry proper will degenerate into mere rhyming, painting into the worst kind of meaningless *genre*, and music into a shallow display of sound, or 'Musikmacherei' as the Germans appropriately call it. Of this original impulse music had lost hold for a long time, chiefly owing to the destructive influence of the Italian operatic stage of the last century. Even in great composers like Mozart or Haydn, the poetical idea was encumbered by the strict forms of absolute music. My meaning is, to be quite explicit, that they would conceive a melody, perhaps full of sentiment, and certainly full of beauty of sound, and develop it exclusively with a view to displaying such beauties. It was Beethoven who first distinctly felt, and Wagner who first expressed in words, the necessity of a previous 'poetical' impulse to which the forms of music proper would have to yield. The unimpaired vitality of pure instrumental music, on these grounds, is of course obvious, it being altogether a secondary consideration whether the 'poetical basis' be expressed in words or not. Much less is the possibility of poetry as a separate art denied by the above theory. Still it is equally true that where a thorough blending of words and music is effected, and most of all in the drama, the very essence of which is passionate impulse, the common effort of both arts will be of a higher kind than is ever attainable by either in its individual sphere. Both have to resign some of their peculiarities, but both gain new strength and beauty in their supreme surrender. They are not, to adopt the equestrian simile of your contributor, 'two riders on the same horse, where one or the other must ride behind,' but rather like two noble steeds drawing with double force and swiftness the fiery chariot of divine pathos."

The whole error, I will add here, seems to me to arise from the mixing up on the writer's part, of art as a revelation to the inspired individual mind, and art as the result of the labour of generations, with a certain amount of rules and principles not unlike the dogmas of an established religious creed. Every artist, if he wishes to deserve his name, must be a perfect master of these forms and rules, the value of which for the most favourable display of the peculiar powers of the art in question, be it music, poetry, or painting, cannot be overrated. But it must be always borne in mind, that the fire of individual inspiration is of divine nature, and, as such, superior in essence to all the accumulated wisdom and skill of the world, entitling, nay, compelling the true artist to find, if necessary, unknown modes of expression for his new lore. In this sense must also be understood what has been said about Wagner's breaking through the forms of absolute music, which he knows how to apply for his purpose with greater skill, than any other living master, but which he abandons in case of need, and repudiates with the same courage and zeal as Luther and Calvin did the grooves of Popish dogmatism.

A second point of vital importance, raised against Wagner by his enemies, is the alleged absence from his style of melody, which, as it is said, and rightly said, must be considered the most unfailing test of all music. It would of course be useless to assert or prove, *à priori*, a thing the existence of which after all one can believe only to his own sense of hearing. Still, the present author has often tried to account for a phenomenon, which is all the more astonishing to him, as he considers melody the very essence of Wagner's music, and is prepared to point out quite as many specimens of beautiful *cantilena* in *Tannhäuser* or *Tristan* as in *Don Giovanni* or *Il Barbiere*. The causes of this extraordinary want of perception, seem to him to lie chiefly in two important features of Wagner's art, not to mention the intentional ill-will of party-prejudiced hearers, which explains of course everything.

One of these causes is, strange to say, the continuous flow of melodious beauty which characterises our master's creations, and which makes it much more difficult to single out a particular motive in his works, than, for instance, in the Italian opera, where a snatch of fine *cantilena* appears like an oasis in the desert of recitativi secchi. Moreover, in Wagner melody and harmony are so closely connected with the dramatic action, that their separate existence becomes imperceptibly mixed up with the general harmony of the work of art as a whole.

The second cause referred to is the increased importance of Wagner's orchestra, into which a great part of the melodious flow is transferred, so as to give the voice more liberty in rendering the accents of genuine passion. It was only natural that both the bravura-singer and his faithful adherents should retaliate for this breach of privilege by not acknowledging, or, maybe, actually not perceiving the existence of instrumental melody.

But now, I fear, I have tried the reader's patience to the utmost. I will, therefore, without further delay, lead him from the barren heath of controversial discussion to the green pastures of undying fiction, and begin the story of *Lohengrin*.

6.

The story of Lohengrin, Parcival's son, on which Wagner has founded his drama, is a compound of many different elements. The Celtic mabinogion, with King Arthur and his knights, and the mystic symbolism of the Graal, the holy vessel (gradale or sang real, whichever it may be), are mixed up with local traditions of the lower Rhineland, of a knight who arrives in a boat without sail or oar, drawn by a swan. In this form the story appears in a queer collection of riddles, repartees, and legends of various kinds, which are brought into a loose connection by an imaginary prize-singing at Wartburg, where they are laid in the mouths of the most celebrated poets of the period. Our story is supposed to be told by the great minne-singer, Wolfram von Eschenbach, whose representative poem, 'Parcival,' might suggest such an arrangement to the compilator of the 'Wartburgkrieg.' It would be a task of great interest, to dissect this late production into its heterogeneous parts, and also to show how far Wagner has altered and remodelled for his dramatic treatment the main features of his mediæval original. From this, however, we must refrain, and limit ourselves to the consideration of Wagner's poem, as we actually find it, without further inquiries as to its genesis.

The ideal background, from which the joys and sorrows of the human actors in *Lohengrin* are reflected with supernal light, is the conception of the Holy Graal itself, the mystic symbol of Christian faith, or, in a wider sense, of everything divine and great, as it reveals itself to the ecstatic eye of the pure and self-surrendering soul. Such an act of revelation is the subject of the instrumental prelude, which serves our opera as an overture. The prelude, and in a certain sense the opera itself, are based on one melodious phrase—the *Graal-motive*, as we will call it—or one might even say on the change of the two chords (that of A major and F sharp minor) which form the harmonious foundation of this prominent melody. To explain the full meaning of this, we must here add a few words about what, in Wagner's operas, is generally called the (*Leitmotiv*) leading motive or melody. For every important idea or passionate impulse of his characters, Wagner introduces a certain striking harmonious or melodious combination, as the musical complement of their dramatic force. Wherever in the course of the drama this impulse comes into action, we hear at once its corresponding motive, either sung by the voice or played by the orchestra, and in manifold variations, according to circumstances. The opening chorus of the pilgrims, interrupted by the wild rhythms of the Venusberg, as the representative melodies of the good and evil principles, in the overture to *Tannhäuser*, or the Romance in the *Flying Dutchman*, may serve the English reader as examples of leading motives. The great increase of intensity and dramatic unity which is thus effected in the musical conception of a character or idea is of course obvious. A similar repetition of melodies was previously applied, but only in a very occasional and undecided manner, by Weber, Meyerbeer, and others. As a distinct principle of art it is entirely due to Wagner's creative genius.

The prelude to *Lohengrin* opens with a long drawn chord of the violins in the highest octaves, continued with the tenderest pianissimo through several bars. It is like the thin white clouds floating in a serene sky, shapeless as yet, and scarcely discernible from the ethereal blue surrounding them. But suddenly the violins sound, as from the furthest distance, and in continued pianissimo, the Graal motive, and at once the clouds take form and motion. Our inner eye discovers a group of angels as they approach us, slowly descending from the height of heaven, and carrying in their midst the holy vessel. Sweetest harmonies float around them, gradually increasing in warmth and variety, till at last, with the fortissimo of the full orchestra, the sacred mystery in all its overpowering splendour is revealed to our enchanted eyes. After this climax of religious ecstasy the harmonious waves begin to recede, and with their ebbing motion the angels gradually, as they have come, return to their celestial abode. Such was, according to Wagner's own indication, the poetical, or one might almost say pictorial, idea which suggested the sublime harmonies of his prelude, and never have the sweetnesses and shudderings of Christian mysticism been more fully expressed than in this triumph of instrumental music.

The fresh allegro at the opening of the first act, leads us back from the sphere of transcendental inspiration into the stream of actual life, and when the curtain rises we see King Henry of Germany surrounded by his feudal vassals and retainers, on a meadow by the side of the Scheldt, near Antwerp. He has assembled the nobles of Brabant, to call on their faithful services against the savage Hungarians, the most dangerous enemies of the empire, and at the same time to mediate in their internal dissensions. The cause of these troubles we hear from the mouth of Count Telramund, a great noble, who accuses Elsa, Princess of Brabant, of having murdered her infant brother during a solitary walk, from which she alone returned, pretending to have lost sight of him in the wood. The motive of this black deed he finds in Elsa's affection for a secret lover, with whom she hopes to share the rule of the country after her brother's death.

This rule, however, Telramund claims for himself, on the ground of his having been chosen by the late duke as Elsa's husband, although the proud maiden spurned his addresses. He also alleges that his present wife, Ortrud, is a scion of the old heathenish Dukes of Friesland, who once reigned over the country. The musical part of this scene is treated in a kind of continuous arioso, resembling most the recitativo obligato of the regular opera, but showing an immense progress upon it as regards power and accuracy of declamation. Telramund's impeachment of Elsa reminds us in its simple grandeur of the grave accents of the antique drama. Of leading motives we may mention that representing the king, which consists of a kind of fanfare, and throughout occurs in the key of C major.

At the king's command Elsa now appears before him, accompanied by a few plaintive notes of sweet melodiousness in the orchestra. They soon pass over into a new theme, which might be called the *dream-*

motive, for it is to its strains that Elsa relates, how a knight of heavenly beauty has appeared to her in a trance, promising his assistance in defending her innocence. The same knight she now chooses for her champion in the ordeal which has been granted by the king on Telramund's demand. Here again the different passions of the chief characters—Telramund's hatred, Elsa's unshakable confidence, the king's compassion, and the echo of these feelings in the hearts of the multitude—are rendered by the music in the finest *nuances*. The dramatic climax is reached when after the second call of the herald, and during Elsa's fervent prayer, there suddenly appears, first in the far distance, but quickly approaching, a boat drawn by a white swan, and in it, leaning on his shield, a knight as Elsa has seen him in her vision. The change from doubt and wildest astonishment to joy and triumphant belief, as expressed in a choral piece of the grandest conception, makes this scene one of the greatest effects dramatic music has ever achieved, and one is not astonished at reading of the shouts and tumults of enthusiastic applause, with which the impulsive Italian audience greeted the appearance of Lohengrin at the first performance of the opera at Bologna.

It ought also to be mentioned that a great part of this overpowering impression is due to the masterly arrangement of the scenic effect, as it is prescribed in its minutest details by the composer himself.

As soon as Lohengrin leaves his boat, a perfect calm follows the outbreak of clamorous joy, and every one listens in respectful silence as he bids farewell to the swan, his faithful guide through the perils of the deep. After this Lohengrin loudly declares the falseness of Telramund's accusation, and asks Elsa's hand as the prize of his valour to be exercised in her defence. But before the battle begins she must promise him never to ask a question about his being or the place from whence he came to her rescue. With this demand of implicit belief we have reached the tragic keynote of the drama, and its importance is musically indicated by a new melody of gravest rhythmical structure, the *motive of warning*. When Elsa grants and promises everything in self-surrendering confidence, Lohengrin himself, who hitherto seemed surrounded by inapproachable sublimity, is overcome by her sweet innocence, and breaks out in the passionate words of " Elsa, I love thee!"

Here again the effect of the musical interpretation leaves any description in words far behind. The rest of the act is chiefly taken up by Lohengrin's easy victory over Telramund, and a grand *ensemble* expressive of triumphant joy, which in its structure resembles the traditional form of the finale.

When the curtain rises a second time we see Telramund, whose life has been saved by his adversary's magnanimity, and Ortrud lying prostrate in despairing hatred on the steps of the royal palace, the illuminated windows of which, combined with the festive noise of a banquet, increase the dreary darkness outside. The ensuing duet is musically founded on a new motive, which is meant to represent the evil principle of heathenish hatred and revenge, as opposed to the heavenly purity of the Graal-motive. For Ortrud now discloses herself as the representative of old Friesish paganism, who by her falsehood and witchcraft has led her husband to the accusation of the innocent Christian maiden. We confess that the introduction in a by-the-way manner of the two great religious principles seems to us not particularly happy, and it cannot be denied that the character of Ortrud herself, although grand in its dramatic conception, has both in its musical and poetical treatment, slightly suffered through this unnecessary complication of motives. Her plan of revenge is founded on the prohibited question about Lohengrin's identity, the asking of which she knows to be fatal to his bride. When Elsa soon afterwards appears on the balcony, Ortrud is pityingly admitted into her presence, and repays the kindness of her protectress by beginning at once to sow the seed of doubt in the innocent heart of her victim.

The following scene contains a grand display of scenic effect in the bridal procession of Elsa, which in slow gravity moves down from the palace to the cathedral, accompanied by the most charming strains of both chorus and orchestra. In this masterly way of illustrating the deeper meaning of a dumb ceremony by a kind of decorative music, Wagner's art and dramatic vocation are shown almost as much as in the stronger accents of passion. Among the ladies in attendance we also discover Ortrud, and at the moment when Elsa is going to enter the cathedral, she steps forward and claims the first entrance for herself, covering her enemy at the same time with insults about the dark origin of the knight of the swan.

The scene is evidently suggested by the quarrel of the two queens in the Nibelungenlied, and, although fine in itself, loses somewhat by its parallelism with the one next following, when Telramund suddenly appears and accuses Lohengrin of having been victorious by the means of hellish witchcraft, daring him at the same time to lift the veil of mystery hanging around him. Lohengrin proudly contemns the slander of an outlaw, appealing to Elsa as his sole judge on earth; and, after she has expressed her unshaken confidence, the twice interrupted procession reaches its destination.

The third act introduces us into the bridal chamber of the newly-united pair. It begins with the outpourings of unimpaired love and happiness. But soon the evil seed of doubt, sown by Ortrud's calumnious insinuations, begins to grow. In all her bliss Elsa feels there is something strange standing between herself and her lord, embittering the sweetness of her love with secret misgivings. The way in which this at first shy and subdued feeling is worked up gradually to the pitch of irrepressible curiosity is a masterpiece of psychological characterisation. The calming and imploring words of her saviour and lover, accompanied by the solemn repetition of the motive of warning—nay, even the heroic feelings of her own heart, that wishes to share any possible dangers, are with womanly logic turned into arguments for asking a question, which must lead to the certain misery of both. At last, just when she has uttered the fatal words, Count Telramund rushes into the room with two other assassins, but, is easily slain by Lohengrin's sword, which Elsa hands to her husband.

The last scene shows again the same meadow by the Scheldt as in the first act. King Henry and his vassals are preparing for their departure to the war. But their knightly joy is interrupted by the corpse of Telramund being carried into their presence. Soon Elsa and, after her, Lohengrin appear. By his wife's unfortunate rashness he is now compelled to disclose his origin and name, as Lohengrin Parcival's son, the Knight of the Graal. The piece in which this is done, showing the Graal-motive in its fullest development, and the impressive melody of his parting song, are amongst the most beautiful parts of the opera. The next following incident is, we must confess, not quite satisfactory, and almost seems to verge on the melodramatic. For suddenly Ortrud turns up and tells the astonished audience that the swan, which reappears in the distance, is no other than Elsa's brother, who has been bewitched by herself into this form, but would have been released without his sister's indiscretion; now he is doomed for ever. But in this last emergency the divine power intervenes again. Lohengrin kneels down in silent prayer, and when he rises the swan has disappeared, and a beautiful youth, the Duke of Brabant, stands by his side. Elsa flies to his embrace, and dies in his arms; while the boat of Lohengrin, drawn by a white dove, and accompanied by the plaintive notes of the Graal-motive in A minor chords, disappears in the distance.

This is the end of Wagner's *Lohengrin*. We have tried to convey a clear idea of its poetical and musical structure to the reader's mind, as far as language can express at all the effects of an art, which by its very essence frustrates an adequate description by words. We have readily acknowledged the high beauties of the work, without concealing its faults and shortcomings. In the history of the opera it marks an immense progress upon its own and any other author's previous works, by the comparative emancipation of its means of expression from the forms of absolute music, by the greater unity and force of dramatic characterisation as brought about by what we called the leading motive, and lastly by the richness and beauty of its melodious and harmonious combinations. *Lohengrin* has carried the name of its author to Italy, the land of song, and one would hail it with welcome, if the knight of the swan were equally destined to be the champion of the music of the future in this country.

II.

The Song.

It is old and plain;
The spinsters and the knitters in the sun,
And the free maids that weave their thread with bones,
Do use to chant it: it is silly sooth,
And dallies with the innocence of love
Like the old age.

Twelfth Night; or, What you will.

CHAPTER II.

FRANZ SCHUBERT.

1.

In glancing through the history of genius, we notice in many cases a strange coincidence between its individual character and the soil from which it takes its origin, and by which its growth is supplied with the most appropriate nourishment. Sometimes it must be confessed, Providence seems to act in a most severe and arbitrary manner; but it will almost always be found, that even the harshest treatment ultimately redounds to the purified regeneration of its seeming victims. Dante was banished from his beloved Florence by the hatred of political enemies, but the personal sting of revengeful invective forms one of the grandest features in his divine poem. "The United States," Baudelaire says, "were to Edgar Poe a vast prison, a wild country, barbarous and gaslit." True, to some extent; but would he, in a more congenial atmosphere, have been able to stamp upon his creations that anathematic inscription of "Never a chance," which forms their indescribable charm?

Schubert's nature was not of a kind to receive additional zest from combating with opposition and envy. His impulsive genius would have withered in the cold thought-stricken atmosphere of the north; and we may call it his first and greatest piece of luck, to have been born in the very centre of warm-blooded south German life, at Vienna on the 31st January, 1797. His father was schoolmaster of the parish of Lichtenthal in that city, and his two matrimonial engagements were blessed with that fertility of propagation, which seems to be the enviable lot of this in many respects peculiarly favoured class. His offspring by his first wife amounted to fourteen children both male and female, of which fortunately only four boys and one girl reached the years of discretion, our composer being the youngest amongst his brothers. The connection was altogether not of a very elevated kind, the first Mrs. Schubert having risen from the kitchen to her more dignified position at the head of the schoolmaster's table. The whole family were more or less connected with the teaching business; besides our composer's father, his uncle, his brother-in-law, two of his brothers, and, for a short time, he himself followed the same calling. There was one great advantage which the boy Franz derived from these, anything but brilliant circumstances, which was his becoming acquainted from his earliest childhood with the art of his choice. At that time it was the duty of a schoolmaster, to impart to his pupils the first elements of vocal and instrumental music, and Schubert the father possessed a more than usual knowledge of this art. His sons, as a matter of course, had the benefit of his instruction; and we are told, that at the age of eight, Franz was able to take the second violin part in duets with his father. There are extant some notes from old Schubert's hand, which, although written at a much later period, throw a stray beam of light on the morning hours of an awakening genius. "When he was five," the father says, "I prepared him for elementary instruction; at six I made him enter my school, where he was always the first amongst his fellows." This noble zeal in the acquiring of useful general knowledge, we are obliged to confess, abated very soon. But another feature of his character which was to last him through life we find strongly indicated in this sketch. "At this age already," father Schubert continues, "he used to be very fond of society, and was never more happy than in the midst of a number of joyous friends."

Finding himself soon unable to keep pace with the rapid progress of Franz's musical talent, his father sent him to one Michael Holzer, organist of the Lichtenthal parish, who was to give him lessons on the piano and organ, and also to introduce him into the intricacies of harmony and thorough bass. This master also soon discovered the unusual gifts of his new pupil. Lovers of anecdote will be delighted to know that one day good old Mr. Holzer was heard to exclaim (his disciple working out in the meanwhile the theme of a fugue on the piano):

"He has all the harmony I wanted to teach him in his little finger; whenever I was going to tell him anything, he was sure to know it already."

The next important step in our hero's musical apprenticeship, is marked by his obtaining a place as soprano chorister in the imperial '*Capelle*,' with which was connected a scholarship at one of the best municipal schools of Vienna, called the 'Stadtconvict.' In October, 1808, Schubert, with several other competitors, presented himself for examination before the conductors of the *Capelle*, Salieri and Eybler. His costume was in accordance with the limited means of his father, anything but *recherché*, and excited at first the hilarity of the other boys. He wore, it seems, a huge light grey coat of undefinable shape, suggesting the idea of flour-dust in the minds of his fellow-competitors, who playfully called him the "little miller." But these untimely jokes soon ceased, when the little miller raised his little voice and began to sing at first sight the most difficult pieces, and also answered all questions about harmony and thorough bass with astonishing sagacity, so that the vote in his favour was given unanimously. It is likely that most of the boys then present lived

K

to witness the triumphs of those other "miller songs," which were to gain immortal fame for their author in the wider arena of both hemispheres.

Schubert was admitted into the 'Stadtconvict' chiefly on the grounds of his beautiful soprano voice, but his considerable skill on the violin, acquired in his father's house, opened to him at the same time the little orchestra connected with that school. Soon he was raised to the dignity of honorary conductor of his fellow-pupils. In this way he became practically acquainted with the treasures of German symphonic literature, and revelled in the melodious beauties of Haydn and Mozart, while the works of his great contemporary, Beethoven, filled him from the first with reverential awe. In other respects the progress of Schubert's studies was less satisfactory. Music had engrossed his intellectual being so entirely, that time and interest for mathematics, classics, and other branches of useful knowledge, as taught at the school, were entirely wanting. When, in 1813, his childish treble began to break, and he had to give up his appointment as a chorister in consequence, Schubert did not avail himself of the permission to continue his general studies at the 'Stadtconvict.' He returned to his father's house, where, for the next three years, he was employed as assistant usher in "teaching the young idea how to shoot," in so far as such shooting may be directed by the oracles of the spelling-book and similar sources of elementary wisdom.

The life of Schubert during his stay at the 'Stadtconvict' does not essentially differ from that of ordinary schoolboys. His greatest trouble seems to have been a state of chronic impecuniosity, with occasional acute attacks of the same evil. During one of these, he writes to his brother Ferdinand the following piteous begging letter, in which his undisturbable good humour is displayed in the sly manner, characteristic also of his riper years: "Let me come to the point at once," he exclaims, "without keeping you in suspense. I have been pondering over my situation for a long time, and find it to be quite tolerable on the whole; it would, however, seem to allow of an occasional slight improvement. You know, by experience, that a fellow would like at times a roll and an apple or two, especially if after a frugal dinner he has to wait for a meagre supper for eight hours and a half. The few groschen that I receive from my father are always gone to the devil the first day, and what am I to do afterwards? 'Those who hope will not be confounded,' says the Bible, and I firmly believe it. Supposing, for instance, you send me a couple of kreutzers a month, I don't think you would notice the difference in your own purse, and I should live quite content and happy in my cloister. St. Matthew says also that whosoever has two coats shall give one to the poor. In the meantime, I trust you will lend your ear to the voice, crying to you incessantly to remember your poor brother Franz, who loves and confides in you."

A more serious inconvenience arising from Schubert's continual want of funds, was the impossibility of procuring a sufficient amount of music paper, necessary to reap the harvest of melodious and harmonious ideas, with which he began to be inspired at this early period. It would be difficult to realise the tragicomic significance of this situation. Imagine a man in the midst of all the riches of the valley of diamonds, but without the means of carrying the useless pelf to inhabited quarters, and you may understand to some extent the despair of this youth, on whom the muse had showered her highest gifts, forgetting only to provide him with the clumsy necessaries of earthly existence. In this particular case we are told that friendship soon stepped in and supplied the young composer with the practical implements of his art.

With this we touch upon an important element in Schubert's life, viz., his strong feeling for the charms of friendship. From the impulsively lyrical character of his works, one might expect that all the fibres of his heart would have tended towards that half of mankind, from which the strongest and purest feelings take their origin, and to which they reciprocally appeal most. But, no; we shall have to mention on more than one occasion the ties of real friendship, which joined him to a great many contemporary artists and poets, while on the other hand the influence of what Goethe calls the "eternal feminine" seems to have been all but wanting, if we except a few ephemeral attachments of a slight order. Schubert even used to chaff his friends on the subject of their numerous *liaisons*, and often received them with the ironical question: "Which one is it now?" The most important connection formed by him during his school time, was with his principal master, the conductor of the imperial *Capelle*, Salieri. The numerous productions of this extraordinary man, like *Le Donne Litterate* and other operas, have long been forgotten, but his name has acquired an unenviable notoriety by his mean intrigues against his great rival, Mozart, whom, according to a rumour current at the time, he was even accused of having poisoned. There is scarcely a greater contrast imaginable than that existing between the old Italian formalist, who, after a stay of nearly half a century at Vienna, had not given up a tittle of his national peculiarities, and young Schubert, with his buoyancy, and essentially German type of genius. Still the maestro seems to have felt instinctively the great though heterogeneous qualities of his pupil, and did all in his power to encourage him. Whatever the personal character of Salieri may have been, he undoubtedly possessed the gift of attaching to himself the love and veneration of his pupils, among whom we count men of eminency, like Hummel, Moscheles, and many more. Schubert also remained always devoted to his old master, and, at the fiftieth anniversary of Salieri's entering the Imperial service, we find his name on the list of those celebrating the day by compositions written for the occasion.

And now I would fain introduce the reader to another, the last scene of this man's life, which tells its own tale of impressive morality. We find it in the autobiographical sketches of Moscheles' life, which, some time ago, have been arranged and published by the loving and skilful hand of his widow. On returning to Vienna, after a long absence, Moscheles was told that his revered master, Salieri, was lying dangerously ill in a public hospital. He at once applied for the necessary passport from Salieri's daughter and the hospital authorities. This permission seems to have been got with some difficulty, there being scarcely any one admitted to the patient, who himself did not care to receive many visitors. "Our meeting," Moscheles says, "was sad to the utmost. I was terrified by his looks. He spoke only in abrupt sentences about his imminent death. At last he burst out, 'Although I know this to be my last illness, I can assure you, on my honour, that there is nothing in that absurd rumour; you know—Mozart—they say I have poisoned him. No, no; nothing but malevolence, malevolence! Do go, dear Moscheles, and tell the world that old Salieri has said this to you on his death-bed.'"

Moscheles adds, that he withdrew in haste, in order to hide his tears. There is, indeed, something indescribably touching and awful in the last words of this dying man. Haunted by revengeful visions, he tries to defend himself in his violently uttered broken German, against the unjust suspicion of a physical crime, while perhaps his inmost soul was smitten with the consciousness of a wrong of blacker dye: poisonous envy and obdurate resistance against the revelations of genius.

Returning now to Schubert's career, we have to go back several years, in order to witness the first indications of his creative power. If we may believe his brother Ferdinand, he wrote his first extensive piece for the pianoforte, a 'Fantasia for four hands,' at the age of thirteen, and his first song, the 'Klagegesang der Hagar,' the 'Complaint of Hagar,' in the following year, not to mention a number of less important productions, which seem to belong to a still earlier date. This precocious development of Schubert, marvellous as it may seem, is still surpassed by his astonishing fertility, which also began to manifest itself at an early period of his life. The year 1812, the fifteenth of his life, gave birth to the following compositions: one Salve Regina, one Kyrie Eleison, one trio for pianoforte, violin, and violoncello, two quatuors for string instruments, two overtures, one andante with variations, thirty minuets, and, strange to say, only one song. And this year was by no means an unusually fertile one. In overlooking the catalogue of Schubert's compositions, the titles of which fill alone something like forty odd pages, and which comprise all the different forms of musical art from the valse to the grand opera, one feels inclined to think that the mere copying out of such a quantity of notes would require a lifetime. Indeed, his nine symphonies and seventeen dramatic works, partly or completely finished, might be considered a satisfactory result of the sixteen years over which his creative period extended. Nevertheless, these works are of small importance, compared with the chamber music and the inexhaustible treasures of song, which have been, and are still being, rediscovered amongst the lumber of amateurs' libraries and publishers' waste-paper baskets. We shall have to consider hereafter how this almost unnatural superabundance of inventive ease acted on the general character of Schubert's creations. In one case it proved absolutely fatal to his productions; I am speaking of his numerous attempts at dramatic composition.

Schubert's first effort in this direction dates as far back as the 'Stadtconvict.' One of the chief attractions of the young student's holidays was the imperial opera, with its unrivalled orchestra and excellent singers.

Here he was impressed by the charming melodies of Weigle's *Swiss Family*, and the stern grandeur of Gluck's and Cherubini's antique heroes and heroines. The elegant graces of Boildieu's *Jean de Paris* also moved him sympathetically. As might be expected, Schubert soon was filled with competitive zeal, and decided upon composing an opera of his own. Unfortunately his choice of a libretto fell upon a *féerie* by Kotzebue, the well-known prolific playwright, called *Des Teufels Lustschloss*, the *Palace of the Devil*. The silly words of this farce he now began to set to music with his usual *verve*. The work was finished in no time, but never saw the light of the stage, and as far as we may judge from our composer's coeval works, and from the miserable stupidity of the words, the world has lost little by this neglect. Indeed, we should scarcely mention the juvenile production at all, if it did not quite as distinctly as Schubert's later works, show his vital deficiencies as a dramatic writer.

We have stated before that after Beethoven's reformatory influence, as manifested even in the works published at that time, a reconstruction of musical art was possible only on a strictly poetical basis. This principle, of course, applies foremost to the drama, which is the highest result of music and poetry combined. A dramatic composer, therefore, had to be particularly careful in choosing the poetical basis on which to construct, and according to the conditions of which to fashion his melodies. For this purpose he required more a keen perception of the dramatic bearing of characters and situations than a surplus store of melodious combinations, which, on the contrary, might, and in Schubert's case did, make him careless in choosing the words, on which the beauty of his tunes seemed so little to depend. In consequence, the firm, not to say harsh emphasis of dramatic expression, so essential to the composer of operatic music is, in Schubert's operas, drenched and crushed by the incessant flow of cantilena; and even his genius cannot atone for the almost incredible silliness, under which most of his libretti labour. Besides this, Schubert's art is always expressive only of his individual feeling, and all but void of that broadness and objectivity of emotional rendering by which alone the progress of an action can be illustrated. His operas, therefore, wherever they have been acted, have earned but scanty applause. During his lifetime this might be accounted for by the general neglect from which his works had to suffer at the hands of purblind contemporaries. But even after his death, when an admiring posterity tried too late to atone for this injustice, it has proved an impossible task for his most devoted worshippers to persuade themselves and the world that the unrivalled "singer of songs" was an equally great composer of operas. Even the performance of *Alfonso and Estrella*, the ripest fruit of Schubert's dramatic muse, which took place under Liszt's masterly leadership, could not obtain more than a *succès d'estime* from an audience of enthusiastic admirers. Quite otherwise, where these flowers of lyrical growth were transferred from the stormy seat of dramatic action into the more congenial atmosphere of the concert-hall. Here the audience do not expect a rapid progress and change of incident, and can rest with delight on the magic charms of Schubert's melodies.

The present writer remembers with delight having taken part, when a student at Leipsic, in the concert rendering by amateurs of one of Schubert's prettiest operettas, called *Der häusliche Krieg*, Anglicè *Domestic Warfare*. The book is written by J. F. Castelli, a prolific writer of all kinds of ephemeral literature, who died not long ago at Vienna. It is certainly silly enough, but shows some technical skill and a great deal of that broad humour which is, or at least was, proverbially attributed to the Viennese bourgeois. As illustrating the lackadaisical manner in which Schubert carried on important matters, it may be quoted that he never thought it worth while to acquaint Castelli with the fact of his having set the libretto, although the two used to meet frequently. The following short sketch will be sufficient to give an idea of what the plots of this and, we might say in a generalising way, of most of Schubert's operas are like:—Count Heribert of Lüdenstein, a great feudal lord, accompanied by his noble retainers, has left his castle for a crusading expedition to Jerusalem. His lady does not approve of the absence of her lord, neither are the spouses of the other knights edified by their husbands' pious dispositions. In consequence, when the imminent return of the weary wanderers from the Holy Land is announced, the ladies enter into a solemn league and covenant to receive them with the semblance of coldest indifference. The knights unfortuately are informed of this trick by a young foot page, who has been present at the ladies' parliament in disguise, and they resolve at once to beat their fair enemies with their own weapons. The first meeting of the reunited couples is therefore more than reserved, and the knights, under the pretence of a sacred vow, which forbids them all intercourse with their better halves, resort at once to the banqueting-hall, where they intend to celebrate the occasion according to their lately acquired bachelor habits. This homœopathic treatment soon begins to take effect on the female mind. The ladies are not a little amazed at the consequences of their rash conduct, and their sorrow is by no means abated, when they are informed of an additional vow taken by their husbands, while in peril of death from the hands of the Turks, to the effect that after a short rest at home they will return to their sacred duties in the Holy Land and remain there for the rest of their lives. The strict fulfilment of this vow—the ladies are told—can only be modified by their taking up arms themselves, and sharing with their husbands the dangers of a long campaign. By this time they have given up all their former ideas of proud defiance, and express unanimously their willingness to give the demanded proof of fond devotion. The last scene shows them all, arrayed in knightly attire, and ready to follow their lords whithersoever. By this heroic conduct the hearts of the crusaders are softened at last. They now explain the whole transaction and express in a final chorus their desire to return to the state of submissive allegiance beseeming good husbands. It need scarcely be added that they are most kindly received by their fair enslavers, who harmoniously join their voices in the expression of reconciliation and universal joy, which concludes the piece.

The style of this dramatic framework, the reader will perceive, is not of a very elevated order, and the dialogue in which the action is carried on, bears the same marks of childish and frequently coarse jocularity. Yet there are in it some amusing and, for the musician, eminently suggestive situations, and wherever an opening for the expansion of lyrical feeling offers itself, Schubert has poured out the abundant gush of his sweetest melodies, raising the hearer, as if by magic, from the commonplace situation of the piece into the sphere of an ideal world. But the very charm of these lyrical intermezzi shows the composer's want of dramatic self-constraint. He considered the opera, as he did indeed all other forms of musical art, as the playground of his immediate lyrical impulse, and wrote in consequence only *enlarged songs*, whether he might call them symphonies, or disguise them as dramatic utterances. The difference between subjective and objective production was entirely hidden to him. In this way we have to explain the want of unity and concentration and the enormous length (Schumann calls it "heavenly") which mar the effect of most of Schubert's larger works. It is always he himself who speaks and feels; and as there is no end of what he has to express, he forgets that even the most heavenly language may exhaust the hearer's receptivity.

We have now to return to a period of Schubert's life, greatly anterior to the events anticipated in our deviatory remarks. He has just left the 'Stadtconvict' and made his entrance into life, with no resources except the treasures of his genius. These not being easily convertible into the coin of the land, he saw himself compelled to earn his bread as best he might. We have mentioned before, how he returned to his father's house, whom he assisted in the drilling of his pupils. We can imagine how intensely his sensitive and retiring nature must have suffered amongst a boisterous herd of uneducated urchins. There were, however, lighter points in this sombre picture. His father and several of his brothers were, as we have seen, industrious worshippers of the 'divine art,' and already, during Franz's schooltime, there existed a Schubert family quartett, in which the father played the violoncello, the two brothers, Ignatz and Ferdinand, the first and second violin, and our composer the viola. It is told that Franz, being the youngest, but by far the most musical member of the party, used invariably to notice the mistakes that were made. In case of his father being the culprit, he generally remained silent in the first instance, and only, when the mistake was repeated in the parallel passage, he used to interrupt the proceedings with the modest remark: "I think,

Sir, there must be something wrong here," whereat worthy old Schubert corrected his mistake without a word of contradiction. The enormous advantage which Schubert derived from the musical atmosphere of his surroundings is evident. He always was sure to find an appreciative and, to some extent, critical audience for his own works, which increased with every year in number and beauty. The hearing of his own music offered at the same time an opportunity for pruning and shortening, of which Schubert, however, availed himself not as much as might be desired. Many important compositions belong to this period, amongst others, the beautiful, so called tragic symphony (which title, by the bye, seems a decided misnomer, the work being, on the contrary, rather of a gentle and serene character). It was written in 1816 for the 'Society of Dilettanti,' which had taken its rise from the original family quartett of the Schuberts, increased by their numerous friends.

It was also about this time that Schubert received the first substantial reward of his artistic labours. He was commissioned to write the cantata of *Prometheus* for a university festival, and the honoraire was fixed at the moderate sum of 100 florins in *paper money*, a figure which, taking into account the state of the Austrian finances at that time, dwindles almost into nothingness. Nevertheless, he carefully commemorates the fact in his diary: " To-day for the first time I composed for money."

We also hear of a mass of Schubert's being played and sung under his own direction at the parish church of Lichtental, at which performance the soprano part was taken by a young lady of the name of Theresa Grobe. She had a beautiful voice, and it is said that the interest which our composer took in her, was not of an exclusively artistic kind. However this may be, the affair led to nothing more than perhaps a fugitive romantic attachment. Theresa soon afterwards married a master baker, and the practical wisdom of her choice is brought to indubitable evidence by the fact, that a short time ago she was still enjoying a blooming old age at Vienna.

Of infinitely greater importance, though much smaller in bulk than the enumerated compositions, is a work, which more than any other has proved the source of what little affluence and fame its author enjoyed during his lifetime. That its popularity has not abated since then, the reader will admit, when I pronounce its name the 'Erlking.'

I should like to mention a few circumstances bearing upon the horoscope of so important a creation. Spaun, one of Schubert's intimates at the time (*i.e.* the end of 1815,) tells us, that the whole piece was written in one afternoon. Schubert read the verses once or twice, and almost instantaneously conceived and arranged his melody. When Spaun, who had left the room, re-entered after a short time, he found his friend noting down the music out of his head.

This enormous rapidity of Schubert's production is another characteristic of his talent. There is an anecdote of a similar kind connected with another song of his. One Sunday he was sitting with several boon companions in a tavern near Vienna, called by the ominous name of the 'Beer Sack'. One of them had a book of poetry with him, and Schubert, glancing through its pages, suddenly exclaimed: "I have a nice melody in my head, if I could only get a piece of ruled paper." Some staves were drawn on the back of a bill of fare, and amidst the din of shouting guests, running waiters, and tinkling harps, the heavenly melody of the 'Serenade' was conceived.

To return to the 'Erlking,' it was as soon as finished taken to the 'Stadtconvict' and sung the same evening to the pupils, first by the composer himself and afterwards by one of his friends. The young critics were rather taken aback by the drastic effects of colouring in the composition, and particularly expressed their astonishment at the minor second occurring in the outcry of the terrified child, till their music-master Ruczizka explained to them the meaning and poetic necessity of the shrill dissonance.

This was perhaps the first, but not the only time that our composer was taxed with eccentricity, abstruseness, and whatever else the favourite epithets of superior Philistinism may be. He shared in this respect the fate of every great master from Palestrina and Bach, down to Schumann and Liszt, not excepting even the serene and simple genius of Mozart. The verdict of the public at the Paris Conservatoire, after hearing Beethoven's Seventh Symphony, delivered in exclamations of "Il est fou" and the like, may be considered as the representative expression of such narrow-minded malignity.

All this while Schubert was teaching the lowest form of his father's school how to spell. We ask, how his noble soul bore such fetters, in what kind of an attitude our hero sat at this worse than spinning wheel? Upon the whole very patiently. Occasionally his grief may have vented itself in angry demonstrations upon the backs of his pupils; there even exists a vague rumour of his being dismissed from his dignity for thrashing an obstinate, or I would rather believe, a stupid boy with more than usual energy. As a rule, however, the serene calm of his mind remained undisturbed. We possess some fragments of his diary, relating to this period, which express anything but a Prometheus-bound-like feeling.* On one occasion he speaks about a concert, at which he had been enjoying himself, and addresses the genius of Mozart in

---

* The history of the narrow escape of these fragments from being destroyed, as told by the well-known Aloys Fuchs in his 'Schubertiana,' is very curious, and deserves mentioning, as illustrative of the unaccountable neglect with which our composer's most precious relics were left to take care of themselves. "Some years ago" Fuchs relates "I found at the shop of an autograph dealer at Vienna the fragments of a diary, written in Schubert's own hand, with several leaves wanting. I questioned the proprietor about it, and the wretch confessed that, he had given the missing sheets away piecemeal, partly to collectors of autographs, partly to admirers of Schubert. After having expressed my opinion about his vandalism, I took care to save what was left."

hyperpathetic terms. Another time he gives a sentimental description of his meeting a friend in the fields; a further entry describes his visit to a picture gallery, and concludes with the not over original remark, that one ought to see pictures often in order to appreciate them properly.

Upon the whole, the style and spirit of these remarks strike one as rather below than above the average, and the same is the case with most of his literary utterances. Schubert, although belonging through his creative works to the new phase of art, was of a decidedly illiterate turn of mind, and never made a serious effort in later life to fill up the gaps of his early education.

It was in the third year of his painful drudgery as a schoolmaster, that a faint hope of possible release seemed to dawn upon Schubert. The position of director of a musical establishment at Laybach became vacant, and although the yearly emoluments of the place amounted to only five hundred florins at the outside, this seemed to Schubert an El Dorado compared with his actual circumstances. His name appeared on the list of competitors, backed by a favourable testimonial from Salieri, and the warm recommendations of the municipal authorities.

But in vain. Fortune, unlike herself, remained for once unchangeable in her step-motherly treatment of this child of genius. Some one else was elected, and Schubert had to continue as a schoolmaster for another year. At the end of this term, friendship again stepped in and broke the hateful chains.

One Franz von Schober, a young poet, had heard and admired some of Schubert's songs, and being told of the composer's narrow circumstances, persuaded his mother, a rich lady, to take the responsibility for the supply of Schubert's modest wants. On these grounds, the latter but too readily threw up his appointment and became a daily guest in Schober's house. Henceforth he never again bound himself by any fixed engagement.

It is this the second time in our short sketch that we see a friend acting as *Deus ex machiná* in Schubert's distresses, and it may seem appropriate to add here a few words about the numerous interesting men with whom his career became more or less closely connected.

We first of all notice that only comparatively few of Schubert's friends were of his own calling. They mostly belonged to a class of general enthusiasts, who in those halcyon days of political lethargy were not uncommonly found in Austria. A man of this kind would broadly sympathise with all artistic aspirations, and so be able to receive the revelations of genius with a willing heart. Unfortunately he would also be apt to express his own vague longings for the ideal in more or less indifferent verse; and it is in this latter capacity that the student of Schubert's songs reluctantly becomes acquainted with names like Schober, Hüttenbrenner, or Mayrhofer. The last mentioned seems to have been on the most intimate terms with Schubert. For two years they lived together in the same room. Two dramas and a number of songs owe their existence to this Bohemian friendship.

As a rule, poet and composer, were at work together at the same time, and as soon as Mayrhofer had finished a sufficient number of verses, he handed them over to Schubert's desk, who clad them in music with a rapidity, that sometimes made it difficult to keep pace with him. The tragic end of Mayrhofer, although happening long after our composer's death, throws a veil of sadness over this bright picture of youthful enthusiasm.

A hypochondriacal morbidness was from the beginning a prominent feature in the young poet's character, and it seems to have grown with his advancing age. Once in a fit of melancholy despair, he tried to drown himself in the Danube. He was however, drawn out of the water and restored to life, but not to the desire of living. He went on quietly for some time, till in 1836 he was suddenly taken with a violent fear of cholera morbus, then raging at Vienna. In order to escape the dreadful enemy, he made, by a strange but not unprecedented inconsistency of human nature, a second, and this time successful attempt at destroying himself.

Another, and upon the whole more useful class of friends, were singers both of the amateur and professional classes, who interpreted Schubert's songs to Viennese circles, and in this way procured him what little fame and gain was allotted to him in this earthly exile. The most prominent amongst these was Vogl, a popular singer at the Imperial Opera, whose name has been preserved from oblivion by his noble exertions in the service of genius. At first there was some difficulty in drawing his attention to the productions of the obscure beginner, but when once the ice was broken, Vogl ardently enlisted in the task of securing a place to the rising star amongst the established constellations; and to this task he adhered to the end. It was long after the death of Schubert, that the then more than sexagenarian sang the 'Erlking' at a public concert. He soon discerned the dream-like character of Schubert's productiveness, and always used to quote an anecdote in illustration of the state of unconsciousness, or as he called it, *clairvoyance*, in which Schubert wrote his finest works. Finding a song of our composer's, which had been left at his rooms, too high for his voice, Vogl had it transposed, and after a fortnight sang it in a lower key to Schubert, who calmly remarked, " Really that ' Lied ' is not so bad ; whom is it by ? " It is also said that Vogl exerted a beneficial influence on his friend, in making him more careful in the choice of the words for his songs.

With the exception of Vogl, Schubert had but little connection with the musical celebrities of his time. He lived indeed a secluded life, in so far as his own existence lay out of the musical atmosphere of his surroundings ; and from what we know of the compounds of this atmosphere, we can quite understand why his uncombative, not to say indolent nature, shrunk from entering the arena of public contest.

Vienna, at that period, was divided into two hostile camps, consisting of the respective disciples of Weber and Rossini, or, as they preferred to call themselves, the German and Italian schools of music. Apart from these, on a solitary height, stood Beethoven, addressing his utterances more to unborn generations than to ungrateful contemporaries.

Schubert, although thoroughly imbued with the ideal seriousness of German art, was altogether of too easy going a nature to take a decided position in this struggle. He composed a couple of Italian overtures, in imitation of Rossini's brilliant *verve*, and was, on the other hand, perhaps slightly biassed against the German champion, by the arrogant *hauteur* with which Weber is said to have treated the young Viennese composer's dramatic efforts. To Beethoven, Schubert always preserved the attitude of a worshipping disciple. Once or twice he tried to approach him personally, but Beethoven's deafness and growing misanthropy, prevented him from taking much notice of an awkward young man, with nothing particular to recommend him. It was only on his death-bed that Beethoven recognised the congenial flame in the works of the younger composer. Schindler tells us that he gave the dying master, shortly before his end, some books of the just published 'Lieder,' to look through, and that Beethoven expressed his admiring astonishment at the flow of melody, and the richness of harmonious combinations, displayed in their narrow limits.

When last we left him, Schubert had just resolved upon meeting the demands of life with his own resources. But too soon he was to find out the impediments of such a bold undertaking; and seeing that the hundred florins earned by his compositions were not likely to receive a new addition from the same quarter, he saw himself compelled to undergo a new, though modified form of drudgery, that is, to give music lessons. Fortunately he met at the beginning of his career with one of those families, not uncommonly found amongst the Austrian nobility, which take a traditional pride in protecting artistic talent. The head of this family, Count Esterhazy, took a great liking for the young man, and engaged him permanently in the instruction of his young and beautiful wife, and his two daughters, aged thirteen and eleven respectively. During the summer months Schubert often went with the Esterhazys to their country seat, at Zelész, in

Hungary, where he became acquainted with those wild, but wonderfully charming rhythms and melodies of half gipsy, half Magyar origin, which he afterwards embodied in his works. It is said that the beautiful motive in the opening of the 'Fantaisie à l'Hongroise,' was overheard by the composer at the Count's castle, where a kitchen-maid used to hum it over her work.

We also have to record in connection with the Esterhazy family a second tender attachment, the most serious one to which our misogynist was ever subject. At first, it is said, Schubert fell in love with a *femme de chambre* of the Countess, but soon this ephemeral passion was consumed by the purer flame of an ideal love, with which the unfolding charms of his younger pupil, Caroline Esterhazy, inspired him. The inexperienced girl scarcely understood the silent devotion of the awkward artist. Only once it seems to have come to an indirect utterance, when upon the Countess asking him, why he had never dedicated any of his works to her, Schubert exclaimed, in his usual abrupt manner: "What's the use of that, everything belongs to you." In this resolution he persisted, and the dedication to Countess Caroline, which stands on the title page of the Fantasia, in F minor, Op. 103 was added by the publisher after the composer's death.

With the beginning of Schubert's career as an independent musician at Vienna, the biographical part of our remarks has nearly reached its end. Henceforth his existence becomes so void of stirring incidents of any kind, that a continuous narration would appear tedious. Those of my readers whom the subject may interest, I will refer for the most accurate details, to the excellent and comprehensive book on Schubert, by Dr. Kreiszle, to which is affixed a catalogue of his works, with the number and date of their publication. I, for my part, must limit myself here to collecting and grouping together such scraps of anecdotal intelligence, as may enable the reader to discern the outline of Schubert's visible fates and features. Of his works also, I shall only mention those which show a more immediate bearing on the general conditions of musical development.

Schubert's exterior, to begin with the least important point, was anything but prepossessing. His features seemed to show some resemblance with those of Beethoven, without however that Jove-like protrusion of forehead in the greater master's physiognomy, which might make one believe in the phrenologists' bump of ideality. The worst feature of our composer's face was his nose, "tip-tilted"—to use the Laureate's ingenious way of putting it—but, alas! anything but "slender." We also miss in him that sweet bent of mouth, those "beautifully rhymed lips," as Heine calls them, which we admire in the portraits of almost all the great lyrists of different ages and nations. The decided tendency towards growing fat, which manifested itself at an early period of life, gave an additional touch of uncouth awkwardness to Schubert's appearance. Contemporaries mention the splendour and depth of his eye as a retrieving feature, which of course cannot be recognised in the indifferent portraits we possess of him. Upon the whole, we can easily understand that his appearance and social accomplishments did not qualify him to shine in the *salons* of the most refined aristocracy of Europe. Indeed, he shunned as much as possible, and much more than was advantageous to his worldly prospects, the circles in which a Viennese reputation could only be established at that time. He only felt comfortable in the midst of jolly companions, and at the genial board of some *Kneipe* (tavern) where the gifts of Bacchus and Gambrinus circulated freely, sometimes but too freely for the continued steadiness of brains and legs. Be it said here, once for all, that Schubert was never a confirmed drunkard, but occasionally indulged in a glass too much.

In company of this kind he was quite at his ease, and often changed his habitual silence with fits of boisterous mirth and joviality, from which however he soon relapsed into absent dreaming, often increased to a state of creative clairvoyance. To a certain gruffness of manner, Schubert owed the title of 'tyrant' occasionally applied to him by his friends, who, nevertheless, loved him with all the sentimentality of South German youth. There are extant a number of letters exchanged between him and his friends, during the various trips into the provinces, which he made at different times. In these we find displayed all the just-mentioned qualities, mixed with that especially Austrian sense for cheap puns and harmless jocularity to which I have also called the reader's attention on more than one occasion.

At other times, however, we see him give way to a sense of depression but too commonly found amongst those who produce works of art from the depths of their own feelings, and the absence of which would be unaccountable in the singer of the 'Winter-reise.' There were even for him intervals of exhaustion, when the emptiness of his earthly existence overshadowed his soul. In one of his letters addressed to his friend Kuppelwieser, at the beginning of 1824, we find a sudden outcry of sadness, which strikes us by the pathetic truth, we might almost call it beauty, of its expression. "You are good and kind," Schubert says, "and will forgive me for what others might take amiss, but the fact is, I'm the most miserable man in existence. Fancy a man, whose health has been irrecoverably lost, and who by his despair makes it still worse instead of better; fancy, I say, a man, whose most brilliant hopes have come to nothing, and to whom even the delights of friendship and love have proved a source of sufferance and pain; nay, whose enthusiasm for the beautiful threatens to vanish, and then ask thyself if I am not to be pitied.

> Meine Ruh' ist hin
> Mein Herz ist schwer,
> Ich finde sie nimmer
> Und nimmermehr.

> My peace is gone,*
> My heart is sore,
> I never shall find it,
> Ah! never more!

So I might say every day; for every night when I go to sleep, I wish never to wake again, and every morning reminds me of yesternight's sorrow."

In the further continuation of the letter, we are made acquainted with some of the immediate causes of this mournful disposition. "His affairs," Schubert says, speaking of a mutual friend, "and my own are in a bad condition, and we neither of us have any money. Your brother's opera† has been declared unfit for the stage, and my music, of course, has also become useless. Some Berlin composer has set Castelli's opera, *The Conspirators*,‡ to music, and it has been received with great applause. In this way I have composed two whole operas for nothing." In Schubert's diary we find an entry

---

* I quote from Mr. Bayard Taylor's excellent translation of Goethe's 'Faust.'

† *Fierabras*, the libretto of which was written by Joseph Kuppelwieser.

‡ Identical with the '*Domestic Warfare*' analysed by us. The original title, '*The Conspirators*,' had been thought objectionable by the theatrical censor of Vienna, as being referable to political matters.

of about the same date, which displays a sad parallelism with the quoted letter. " My works," he writes there, " are the children of my intellect and sorrow, and those seem to delight the world most which my sadness alone has created."

This despondency was not the effect of constitutional melancholy or morbid affectation. We must, on the contrary, admire the courage and equanimity with which Schubert bore up against the sea of troubles, attacking him from all sides, with more than usual vigour and obstinacy. It is true that almost every one, who sets out on the thornful way to the temple of fame has to suffer from the indifference with which the world looks upon a beginner.

The stern judges, who hold in one hand the key of the gate to immortality, while the other feels the pulse of the sovereign called public, seldom encourage the young artist's first effort, or, to speak without metaphor, publishers are naturally shy of launching the ominous Op. 1 of an unknown composer. But this does not apply to Schubert. His songs were largely circulated in manuscript, and received with increasing applause in all the drawing-rooms of Vienna, and still no publisher could be persuaded to venture upon the purchase of so popular a work as the 'Erlking.' It had to be brought out at last at the expense of the composer's friends. Even when the enormous profits reaped from the sale of his songs by Spina and other Vienna publishers had opened their eyes to some extent, Schubert had constantly to hear ridiculous suggestions as to making his accompaniments easier, and similar miserable devices from the tradesman's point of view.

At various periods of his life he attempted to improve his precarious situation by finding a fixed appointment of some kind, but always in vain. Even the barren honour of being accepted as a member of the "Society of Friends of Music" he coveted without success. On the other hand, it must be confessed that his own easy going and, as far as his worldly affairs were concerned, extremely lazy disposition prevented him from ever taking fortune by the forelock. His indifference to applause and money had become almost proverbial amongst his friends, who had constantly to be on the alert, and use all possible means of persuasion in order to make him keep the most important appointments. Once an advantageous situation as organist at the Imperial chapel was offered to Schubert by Count Dietrichstein, but refused by him for unknown reasons. Perhaps he had resigned himself to poverty by that time, and would not accept a preferment which might interfere with the higher duties of his artistic vocation.

One chief source of income for Viennese composers at that time was the public performance of their works in what were then called 'Academies,' that is, great concerts of instrumental and vocal music.

Perhaps some of my readers have heard of that memorable 'Academie' in which Beethoven's Ninth Symphony was first produced in public, and excited storms of applause. Being unable to hear, the deaf composer had to be turned round, so as to make him realise by the waving of hats and handkerchiefs the effect of his work.

From this kind of public success Schubert was to a great extent precluded by his bashfulness, and also by the fact that he played no instrument as a virtuoso. It is said, that although he accompanied his own songs on the piano most beautifully, he never acquired any remarkable technical skill on that instrument. Only once he appeared in public as the conductor of a concert given by himself. The scheme consisted exclusively of his own works, mostly vocal, and the success was brilliant in all respects. It was going to be repeated by the composer, when his last illness intervened, and extinguished this faint glimmer of ephemeral good fortune.

So lived Schubert, unknown, and scarcely protected against actual want, while others were reaping the fruits of his labour. But shall we therefore pity a man, who all the while revelled in the treasures of his creative ore, and from the very depths of whose despair sprang the sweetest flowers of song? Who would not battle with the iciest blast of the north, if out of storm and snow he could bring back to his chamber the germs of the 'Winter-reise?' Who would grudge the moisture of his eyes if he could render it immortal in the strains of Schubert's 'Lob der Thräne?'

With this we touch upon that side of his genius, upon which his claims to immortality must chiefly rest, I mean his power of embodying his individual feelings in his art, as the result of which power we have to consider his *songs*. But before I can enter more fully into this most important part of Schubert's works, I must ask the reader to accompany me in a short analysis of the historical growth of the song itself, and the peculiar position it takes in both the poetical and musical branches of emotional utterance in Germany. An investigation of the purely literary side of the question will be the more indispensable, as through it a new undeniable proof of the inseparable connection of music and poetry will be afforded. It may indeed be affirmed that the high position, which the song takes at the present day amongst the other forms of musical art, is quite as much owing to the great modern lyrists of Germany, as to the composers who by their works were inspired to commensurate efforts.

2.

Heinrich Heine, in his delightful preface to a new German translation of 'Don Quixote,' occasionally remarks upon the comparative merits of different national contributions to universal literature, and after having awarded the first prize in novel writing to the Spaniard Cervantes, and that in the drama to the Englishman Shakespeare, he apostrophises his own countrymen in the following manner: "And the Germans, what palm is due to them? Well, we are the best writers of songs in the world. No people possesses such beautiful *Lieder* as the Germans. Just at present the nations have too much political business on hand, but after that has once been settled, we Germans, Englishmen, Spaniards, Frenchmen, and Italians will all go into the green forest and sing, and the nightingale shall be umpire. I feel sure that in this contest the song of Wolfgang Goethe will gain the prize." In another place Heine predicts that posterity will couple his own name with that of Goethe, as equally representative of German song, and the present generation already seems but too willing to acknowledge the younger poet's proud claim to this companionship. But besides these two, a third poet might be named of no lesser excellence, and worthy to complete the lyrical triad on the German Parnassus, a poet of indisputable priority as to time, and inferior to neither of his rivals in range and depth of feeling, although his work bears the modest and half anonymous signature of 'The People.' It is indeed to the inexhaustible treasure of their popular songs, more than to any other cause, that the Germans are indebted for the consciously artistic achievements of their great lyrical poets.

There are two points which distinguish the *Volkslied* from, and raise it in literary importance above, the popular utterances of all other nations. As the first, I mention its wide range of topic, which comprises almost all phases of domestic, religious, and political life, in their action on the unsophisticated and very often but too immediately concerned mind of the toiling multitude. One might, in this respect, consider the *Volkslied* as a continual commentary on historical events, in which the types of official saints and heroes frequently reappear in the quaintest distortions. But, side by side with the traces of drollery and satire, we find the expression of deepest sympathy, and an intuitive understanding for the great events of human progress. Nowhere has the indignant resistance of the free-born soul against spiritual fetters resounded more powerfully than in Luther's hymn, *Ein' feste Burg* (which, although, of known origin, by its elementary force and simplicity of feeling, seems to deserve the name of *the* German *Volkslied*, recently granted to it), and other songs of the Reformation period.

We also must not forget the irrepressible tendency of the German soldier towards celebrating his own and his commander's feats of valour in more or less indifferent doggrel, to which we owe many valuable contributions, from the song of the lanzknecht who "was present" (this assertion of personal autopsy is typical) when they caught the French King at Pavia, down to the ballad of 'Prince Eugene, the noble knight,' and the strongly diluted, but still somewhat racy, patriotic effusions of the great Frederick's grenadier, by father Gleim.* If to these we add the *Wanderlied*, sung by the vagabond scholar and the journeying handicraftsman, and the drinking-song, full of jolly Walter Mapes-like bonhomie, we shall have nearly exhausted the favourite subjects of the popular song, as far as they are attached to the outward occurrences of human life.

But nowhere is the depth and tenderness of the

* I must remind the reader that the *incognito* of the author is not considered by me as an essential feature of the popular in opposition to the artistic song. The two criteria of the 'Volkslied' are, firstly, its actual or past popularity, and secondly, the real or apparent absence of artistic purpose, founded either on genuine naïveté or on the conscious effort of high poetic genius.

German nature displayed to greater advantage than in the true domain of all lyrical poetry, the love-song. It is undeniable that these artless ditties cannot vie with the peculiar sweetness and *verve* of the French *chanson* or the sonorous grace of Tuscan *rispettti* and *stornelli*, any more than a lanzknecht song could equal the weirdness of a Scotch ballad; but it is just this total want of outward effect, and its exclusive reliance on the power of true feeling, which gives its principal charm to the German song, and at the same time makes it so eminently representative of German national character.

I will not encumber the pages of this work with an ever so slight æsthetical sketch of German popular poetry. May I only be allowed to quote, as a specimen of the love-song with which we are here more immediately concerned, the following sad ditty. The reader must not ask me about its author or its presumable date. I only know that I used to hum its melancholy tune, and was impressed by its half-understood symbolism, at an age when all such antiquarian niceties seemed to be utterly irrelevant, as irrelevant indeed as perhaps they in reality are. Printed I saw it for the first time a few weeks ago, in Schuré's charming 'Histoire du Lied.' My translation reproduces the original as closely as possible:

> "Last night I have been dreaming
>   A dream, so heavily,
> In my garden there was growing
>   A tree of rosemary.
>
> " A churchyard was the garden,
>   A grave the flower-bed,
> And from the tree were drooping
>   The leaves and blossoms dead.
>
> " The blossoms I did gather
>   In a golden pitcher withal,
> Till broken quite to pieces
>   From my hands I saw it fall.
>
> " Then saw I tears a-running,
>   And drops as blood so red,
> What can the dream be meaning—
>   Sweet true love, art thou dead?"

The second characteristic feature of the *Volkslied* alluded to, stands in the relation of both cause and effect to the richness and variety of its motives. It is the continual contact and interchange of ideas between the popular and the artistic song. Early traces of this reciprocity we discover in what has been called the first classical age of German poetry, *i.e.*, the time of the Minnesingers. Although the social position of these courtly poets widely severed them from their humbler brethren of the fair and roadside inn, still they never disdained to imbue their fantasy with the ever fresh naïveté of popular feeling. The most charming song of Walter von der Vogelweide, and perhaps one of the sweetest blossoms of erotic poetry, generally called from its suggestive burden 'Tandaradei' is written in the style of what has been named ignominiously "the lower love," but what, in reality, is only the undisguised rendering of preartistic sentiment.

It was thus that the Minnesinger repaid with the additional interest of his genius and refinement, the suggestion he owed to the treasure of the people's feeling, very different in this respect from the accomplished poet of the Langues d'Oc and d'Oil. Both Troubadours and Trouvères borrowed some of their most charming forms, like the Alba, Serenade, and Pastorelle, from rustic song, but under their hands these simple blossoms of the field were forced into an artificial bloom, of great beauty and splendour, but entirely unavailable for the less refined taste of the multitude. The deep chasm opened in this way between Minstrels and Troubadours, natural and refined singers, could not but prove fatal to the creations of both. Courtly poetry, deprived of the ever new pulsation of unalloyed feeling, soon degenerated into a mere worship of abstract form, the petrified specimens of which we still admire in the stately and sonorous, but too often almost meaningless, stanzas of Arnaut Daniel and Folco of Marseilles. The popular muse, on the other hand, left without the guidance and example of her more refined sister, relapsed into grossness, and for a long time lost even the organ of exalted speech in the unintelligible stammering of a low patois.

In Germany, also, the prime of artistic song, as represented in names like Walter von der Vogelweide and Nithart von Reuenthal, was not of long duration. During the fifteenth and sixteenth centuries, poetry passed from the hands of a decaying nobility into those of the rising bourgeoisie, and was treated by the worthy "master singers" very much like another handicraft. A code of rules, under the name of *Tabulatur*, was established, and his increasing proficiency in handling the traditional forms raised the aspiring singer through the different stages of apprenticeship to the dignity of a master and judge. The frequent glimpses of real poetic feeling, visible through the sluggish stream of Philistinism, form the redeeming features in this picture.

But even these were wanting, when Martin Opitz, during the troubles of the war of thirty years, again raised the banner of German poetry, and ushered in the period of second-hand rococo which, in trying to reproduce the dignified graces of the French muse, ultimately tended to expose the hollow affectation of her pseudo-classicism in a Teutonic undress.

In the meanwhile the *Volkslied* went its own way, all but unnoticed by the literati of the day, but preserved from the influences of lassitude and commonplace vulgarity by the mighty events which, from time to time, stirring up the passions of the nation, roused the popular muse to corresponding efforts. I have mentioned before the assistance lent by the poetry of the people to the reformatory movement of the sixteenth century, and I will add here, that in the many beautiful choral melodies used at the present time in the Protestant service, popular tunes of great antiquity, and originally intended for a very different purpose, may be recognised.

It remains to be acknowledged, that a feeling for the charms of the pure source of unalloyed impulse was, even during the most artificial times, never quite lost amongst German poets. The beautiful songs of Simon Dach and Paul Flemming, conceived in the purest strain of popular simplicity, in the midst of the hubbub of both Silesian schools, strike one like the sweet wood-note of a wild bird among a flock of screaming peacocks.

The same consciousness of the great value for poetry of a popular origin, was shown at a later period and in a manner characteristic to himself, by the man who, more than any other, may lay claim to the dignity of a liberator of the muse from conventional fetters. I am referring to a letter from Gotthold Ephraim Lessing, to his friend Nicolai, dated 20th September, 1777. The latter, a publisher, and at the same time a prolific author, of Berlin, belonged to a school of superficial Voltairians who, extending their scepticism beyond the limits of religious inquiry, were apt to consider as barbarous, whatever did not fit into the system of their dry North-German rationalism. Not unlike certain contemporary legislators, Nicolai was prone to place all the evils of this wicked world to the account of the Society of Jesus, and to this idiosyncrasy, combined with a clumsy attack on Goethe's 'Werther,' he owes his place in 'Faust' as "Proktophantasmist," who even on Mount Brocken "scents the Jesuits." In the revived interest for popular poetry which, owing to Herder's meritorious researches, began at that time to spread in Germany, he, of course, discovered only a morbid craving for the dark middle ages, and, in order to ridicule the whole movement, proposed to publish a collection of the silliest possible specimens of old songs, for which he also solicited Lessing's contributions. But here he was to be sorely disappointed. Lessing, in his answer, strongly insists upon the merits of a true song of the people, as distinguished on the one side from the vulgar utterance of the rabble, and on the other from the inane productions of "scholarly rhymesters of the fourteenth and fifteenth centuries." As a model of genuine power, he quotes a broom-maker's song, heard by himself in his childhood from a member of the profession. In order to give the English reader an opportunity of forming his own opinion on a poem, so much extolled by the great critic, I will here insert a translation of the few lines in question, in which unfortunately the racy flavour of the German word "saufen" could, for want of an English equivalent, be rendered but imperfectly. It runs thus :—

> "If I've no tin to get a drop,
> I go and tie some besoms up,
> And go the alleys down and up,
> And hollo: 'Buy my besoms up,'
> To get me tin to get a drop."

The zeal of Herder in discovering the hidden treasures of ancient folk-lore, roused chiefly by the previous similar attempts of Bishop Percy in this country, was, of course, not to be damped by Nicolai's dry scoff. As the final result of his researches, he published specimens of popular song amongst all nations, under the title of the 'Voices of Nations in Songs,' and from the appearance of this work, we may date, to some extent, the rise of a new epoch in poetry. The importance of the book lies perhaps less in the collected material, which, according to the scanty philological resources of the time, leaves much to be desired, as in the great interest, with which the young and susceptible soul of Goethe received the new revelation. Most of my readers will know Goethe's masterly poem of the 'Complaint of the noble Wife of Asan-Aga,' which was smuggled into the volume as a translation from the original 'Morlackisch.'

But the impulse once received was soon to lead to higher efforts. Herder's idea chimed in too well with the general disposition of the time, and the young poet's individual bias, not to be conducive to deeds of greater valour than a clever imitation. For this was the period of "storm and stress" in German literature. The cause of the natural *v.* the artificial, of Shakespeare against French classicism had been pleaded by the mighty voice of Lessing; and Goethe's own early productions in the drama and novel show distinctly enough, which way his genius tended. What was more natural, than that now, when the wide unknown regions of popular feeling were discovered to him, when the lyrical giant touched his congenial mother-soil, his power of song grew irresistible? In this way another stronghold of antiquated prejudice was broken, and a new domain thrown open to the longing of the human heart for impulsive utterance.

I have tried hitherto to sketch the line of progress, which ultimately led to the re-union of popular and artistic song by the greatest poetic genius of modern times. Henceforth the task would devolve upon me, to follow the new form of art on its further course through the bright but passing glow of the romantic school, to its second climax of development, when, under the hands of Heine and his followers, it was to become the exponent of intensest passion and deepest suffering. Many stars of song might be named, like Brentano, Eichendorff, and Lenau, each bright and powerful in its individual sphere. But as I must fear that to the greater number of English readers these names are, and would have to remain, names only, I will limit myself to tracing a few general features, adhering essentially to the nature of German artistic song.

As far as its metrical structure is concerned, the song of Goethe and Heine displays but little difference from its popular source. Take, for instance, the following well-known stanza from one of the songs in Wilhelm Meister:—

"Who never ate with tears his bread,
 Who never passed the night's long hours
Sleepless and weeping on his bed—
 He knows you not, ye heavenly powers,"

and compare it with the above-quoted popular love-poem. The increase of every line by one iambic foot is, of course, quite accidental, and the only additional piece of workmanship consists in the introduction of rhyme into the first and third lines of every verse. But even this is not by any means a necessary requirement of artistic song. The only way, in which the poet could show his formal mastery, and in which indeed it has been shown by representative men, consists in those slight rhythmical *nuances*, mostly of an onomatopoetic kind, achievable only by the hand of genius, and scarcely perceptible to the multitude.

This absence of all artificial effect contains at once a great danger and a still greater advantage with regard to the course of German literature, as distinguished from that of other nations. Let us, for instance, throw a comparing side glance on two of the great English lyrists of the beginning of the present century. Both Shelley and Keats were prone to grapple with the great problems of humanity, and the only style in which such exalted subjects could be treated, naturally tended more towards the Pindaric ode than the simple stanza of the popular song. Hence the wonderful beauty and variety in the structure of their strophes and the elevation of their language; hence also the high standard of modern poetic language in this country which ought to deter the young bard from entering the lists unprepared, or which, at least, makes it easy to distinguish the master from the incompetent blunderer; the danger only being, that undue importance may be gained by sound over sense, by mechanical skill over natural impulse.

Such a danger need certainly not be apprehended in Germany, where the easy flow of the *Volkslied* stanza gave and gives a but too welcome opportunity to the feeling youth, for providing his commonplace amorousness with the additional charm of tolerable verse. But, on the other hand, the simplicity in metre and diction, implied by the popular origin of German artistic song, gave full liberty to its masters, in concentrating the power of their genius on the unfettered expression of their impulsive thoughts, expanding, in this way, the flower-like nature of the *Volkslied* into a creation of highest artistic consciousness.

Last, but not least, I mention the great advantages, which the conciseness of German lyrics offered to the melodies of the composer, and this brings us back to the musical consideration of our theme. We will here also begin with a brief survey of the historical material.

Our remarks about the melodies of popular songs in Germany will be few and short. A classification of individual tunes would, in most cases, prove all but impossible, since the character of their modulations has undergone the influence of consecutive ages; a guess from the known or definable date of words as to the equal age of their musical accompaniments would also, in many cases, be open to serious objections, seeing that one and the same tune has often been used for different poems at different times. Numerous secular tunes have, as we mentioned before, been adopted by both the old and new churches for their purposes, and to these we shall have to recur on a later occasion. As to the general character of the German popular tune, especially in the love-song, it may be said that, together with high beauties of melodious expressiveness, it displays great simplicity, and often monotony, of rhythmical progress, which, combined with the frequently occurring minor keys, is, on the whole, admirably adapted to express the melancholy tone of most of the poems. As to the musical form of the *Volkslied*, I must ask the reader to remember that a strictly strophic treatment is with few, if any, exceptions adhered to, the melody of the first stanza being, without changes of importance, repeated in all the following ones.

Between this and the variegated musical treatment of the artistic German song there is a wide chasm, and, in trying to overbridge it, music itself offers us but little assistance. The only immediate influence of the popular element on the works of Schubert, the first and chief representative of modern song, must be referred to the Sclavonic rather than to his own nationality, and is chiefly discernible in his instrumental compositions.

It is true that the great masters of the last century repeatedly tried their power in the domain of song, but their efforts never proved of long vitality, partly because the poems of contemporary writers contained but little of an inspiring nature, partly, also, because these composers did not fully comprehend the nature of this particular form of art. Mozart, for instance, introduced into his setting of Goethe's 'Violet' a distinct recitative, which, although charming in itself, cannot but appear out of place in these surroundings. Almost the same might, in a modified way, be applied to Beethoven himself; for, although he fully understood the bearing of Goethe's lyrical efforts on the sister art, and, indeed, has anticipated in his settings of the great poet's words, all the essential varieties of treatment, as applied in the artistic song of the present time, still it must be said that the condensed, almost epigrammatic, mode of expression required in the song, always proved a fetter to his grandly dramatic pathos.

But, nevertheless, it was Beethoven who, by urging in his great instrumental works, and particularly in the Ninth Symphony, the demand of a poetical basis of music, reacted inspiringly on his disciple Schubert, and through him on the progressive development of song. I, of course, do not mean to imply that Schubert's lyrical works were originated, or even influenced, by Beethoven's last Symphony, which many of them preceded in time. But it seems that in the mysterious system of reciprocating forces, called economy of nature, the energy of dramatic expression was entirely absorbed by the greatest of modern masters, and the only step in advance which could be made at the time lay in the sphere of subjective passion. To supply this demand, the lyrical genius of Franz Schubert was fashioned and formed by nature's own hand, and it is to the happy coincidence of his birth being almost simultaneous with the *literary* revival of the *Volkslied*, that the artistic song owes its high position amongst the other forms of modern art, and at the same time marks an important step towards the ultimate amalgamation of poetry and music.

In the artistic song so created, we have to consider three different forms of equal importance, all of them known to, and used with success by, Schubert.

The first and simplest of them we will call the " strophic song," because in imitation of the *Volkslied*, it repeats throughout the unchanged melody of the first stanza. As a charming specimen of this kind I quote Schubert's setting of Goethe's 'Haideröslein,' the tender grace of which is inimitably rendered by the melody.

Very different from this is what the Germans call by the untranslatable but easily comprehensible title of 'Durchcomponirtes (literally, throughcomposed) Lied,' in which the melody follows as closely as possible the different feelings expressed by the words, and therefore has to change with the varied sentiments of the single stanzas, artistic unity being preserved either by a recurring motive in the accompaniment, or by the return of the first melody at the end of the song. Schubert's 'Lindenbaum' may be considered as representative of this phase in lyrical music.

A still more progressive tendency is shown in what we will term the "declamatory song." In this we closely approach the border-line of the "music of the future," one important principle of which becomes distinctly recognisable. The vocal part is here changed into a kind of emphasised enunciation, while the accompaniment, raised to a hitherto unknown expressiveness, lets us divine the undercurrent of emotional pathos. Only where the lyrical feeling rises to a climax of intensity, the voice breaks out into a stream of melodious beauty, made doubly impressive by the poetic demand, which it is destined to supply. As a masterpiece of this kind, and as one of the finest songs ever produced, we mention Schubert's 'Die Stadt,' with its marvellous pianoforte bye-play, suggestive of the winds of heaven and the sighs of love forlorn. It is by songs of this order that

Schubert has deserved the name of "le musicien le plus poétique," attributed to him by Liszt, a name which, at the same time, expresses most emphatically his claim to a place amongst the greatest masters of his art.

Schubert died young, "rich in what he gave, richer in what he promised," as the inscription on his tombstone has it. That the height of his creative power was not surpassed, perhaps not reached by him at his death, is shown by the fact that the finest specimens of his lyrical muse are in a posthumous collection of his songs.

The words of nearly half the songs in Schubert's 'Schwanengesang' are by Heine; and one can easily distinguish how the lyrical intensity of that great poet touched the deepest string in the composer's congenial nature. It is difficult to say what might have been the consequences, if the rising fame of the young Rhenish poet had reached the distant Austrian capital sooner. As it was, Schubert saw the 'Buch der Lieder' not long before his death, but just in time to open the vista of a new phase in the development of lyrical music. For it was under the influence of Heine's condensed lyrical pathos, that Schubert abandoned the principle of absolute melodiousness, in which he had earned his greenest laurels, and to which he was led by the bias of his peculiar gift more, than any other master since Mozart. The victory of poetical over absolute music—of the ' Future' over the ' Past '—was gained once more.

3.

We have to add only a few words about our master's dying days. His brother Ferdinand, who nursed him during his fatal illness, has given us a simple but impressive account of his last hours. Schubert had been suffering from a severe indisposition, and had scarcely taken any substantial nourishment for more than a fortnight; at last, on the 11th of November, 1828, his weakness became such, that he had to betake himself to his bed, without, however, suffering much inconvenience beyond an alarming degree of sleeplessness and general exhaustion. During the first two or three days of his illness he tried to get up for a few hours, in order to correct the proofs of the second part of his ' Winter-reise.' Even after the physicians had declared his illness to be typhus fever, the patient was busy with plans for new compositions, amongst which an opera called *The Count of Gleichen* greatly occupied his thoughts. In the meanwhile his illness made rapid progress. On the 18th of November he called his brother to his bedside and said: "Ferdinand, put your ear close to my mouth," adding in a mysterious whisper: "What is going to happen to me?" His brother tried to calm him with hopes of a speedy recovery, but the patient got more and more excited, and repeatedly tried to rise from his bed, believing himself to be in a strange room. When the physician arrived a few hours afterwards and tried to comfort him, Schubert leant his hand against the wall and said in a slow voice: "Here, here is an end of me." These were the last words he uttered; he died at three o'clock in the afternoon of November 19th, 1828. He was buried in the cemetery of Währing, close to where Beethoven lies, although he died in a different parish. This arrangement was made, owing to an incident of Schubert's last illness, which we give in the words of his brother. Two days after our composer's death, Ferdinand writes to his father: "Dear and honoured father, many people have expressed a wish to see our dear Franz buried in the Währing cemetery, and I agree with them, believing this to have been his own desire. On the evening before his death he said to me in a state of half consciousness: 'I implore you to take me to my room, and not to let me lie in this corner under the earth. Dont I deserve a place overground?' I answered him: 'Dear Franz, calm yourself. Believe in your brother Ferdinand, in whom you have always had confidence, and who is so fond of you. You are in your own room, where you have always been, and are lying in your own bed.' Then Franz said again: 'No, that cannot be true; Beethoven is not lying here.' Is not this a sign of his most ardent wish, to be placed near Beethoven, whom he admired so much?"

However this may be, we gladly recognise the significance of the fact of Schubert's resting after death near the master, who in life had been the guiding star of his aspirations.

CHAPTER III.

ROBERT SCHUMANN.

1.

ROBERT SCHUMANN'S place in the history of his art, is generally described as that of the leader of the *romantic* school of music. This name, whether well or ill-chosen, indicates at any rate the relations between his music and the corresponding movement in German literature, known by the same appellation, and it was on these grounds eagerly adopted by Schumann himself. Indeed the whole character of his early efforts is, to a certain extent, explicable only from a literary point of view, and it is also on this close connection with poetical aspirations, that Schumann must rest his claim to the name of (to speak figuratively) the St. John of that important phase of artistic progress which we have called "poetic music," and as the paraclete of which we recognised the gigantic genius of Richard Wagner. It is true that the works of Schumann's riper years disavow (as he did himself by word of mouth) what he then called his youthful eccentricities, and tend to show that his breach with the established form in favour of poetical impulse, had never been of a very serious kind. Still the fact of his original tendency towards what he himself called "the poetry of art" remains unshaken, and is morever attested by his own philosophical writings on the sources and conditions of musical inspiration. It is herefore in the twofold capacity as a composer and as a literary man that we shall have to consider Schumann in the following pages. But first of all we must enter upon a short survey of his youthful doings and longings.

Robert Schumann was born at Zwickau, a small town in the kingdom of Saxony, in 1810, the youngest of five children. His father was the founder and head of a publishing firm of some importance, still existing; at the same time he was a man of considerable taste in literature and art, and himself the author of various works on commercial and other subjects. Milton and Young were his favourite authors, but he equally appreciated the merits of more modern English poets. To a translation of Byron's works, published by his firm, he himself contributed 'Childe Harold' and 'Beppo.' It is generally supposed that poets and artists inherit their talents and inclinations chiefly from their mothers. With our composer the reverse seems to have been the case. While the elder Schumann was decidedly a man of talent in his small way, his wife was of a more practical turn of mind, and eventually showed an almost eccentric aversion against her son's choosing the career of a musician.

About Schumann's early youth there is little to be said. He was considered a kind-hearted, genial boy, with a fair but not astonishing amount of talents; very fond of playing pretty tunes on the piano, but very little inclined to practise in a methodical way, or to trouble his head about harmony and counterpoint. Nevertheless he began composing little melodies at a very early age, and it is also said that he possessed the talent of mimicking certain peculiarities of his friends by particularly striking combinations of sounds; a gift which earned for him great admiration, and indeed opens a prospect to the great achievements of a later period. At the same time he used to try his hand at poetry. Romantic dramas, full of horrors and highwaymen, of his own composition, were performed by Schumann and his friends on an improvised stage, the father looking on all the while and carefully watching the dark and as yet undecided aspirations of his favourite son. If the elder Schumann had lived, the career of our composer would probably have taken a very different turn, and many troubles might have been saved him. It seems that at a very early stage of his son's development, father Schumann recognised, or at least suspected, the great genius struggling in Robert, and actually asked C. M. von Weber to undertake the musical education of the young student. Unfortunately this proposal came for unknown reasons to nothing, and our composer continued at Zwickau in a fair way of becoming a local celebrity, but with very little advantage for his artistic progress. Soon afterwards his father died, and when, at Schumann's school education being finished, the choice of a profession came in question, his widowed mother opposed an obstinate *veto* against her son's entering the career of a *virtuoso*.

We have now to accompany Schumann to the old university town of Leipsic, where he was inscribed in the books of the Alma Mater as a worshipper of Themis, while in reality his heart remained unchangeably attached to the muse. We possess a letter of the young law-student *malgré lui*, written soon after his arrival at Leipsic, to a friend with whom he had been travelling in South Germany, previous to his definite settlement at the university. This document is interesting in many respects, as giving a striking view of his wild oats, which, by the way, were sown at that time by most young men of genius, in the same almost typical manner. This was the period of Friedrich Richter's greatest glory, the halo round the poet's features being still intensified by his recent death. The readers of 'Sartor Resartus' will understand what in Germany is called 'Jean Paulism,' and not be surprised at some hypersentimental eccentricities in the following extracts. In Schumann's case, the disease took the form of a strong tendency towards falling in love in a general way, the then following despair being flavoured with the additional troubles of a chronic lack of cash.

But now for the letter. It is dated the fifth of June, 1828, and runs thus: "My dearest Rosen,—To-day is the nineteenth of June, unfortunately it has taken all this time to continue my letter. Oh! to be with you at Heidelberg. Leipsic is an infamous hole, where one can't enjoy one's life a bit; my money makes rapid progress, much more so than I do at the lecture hall, a remark which is both wise and taken from life, nay, which is more, from my own life." (Thus far the freshman has been prevalent, but now Jean Paul appears in the background.) "Here I sit, without money, and comparing in silence the present with the hours just gone, which I passed with you so delightfully. Musing I stand before your image, and before the whimsical fate which leads men to meet each other from the most distant quarters of the world, only to unite and separate them again. You perhaps are now sitting on the ruins of the old castle, smiling and looking with a joyful heart on the blossoms of June, while I stand on the ruins of my own airy castles and dreams, weeping and looking up to the dark sky of the present and future. However, this letter seems about to grow dreadfully serious, but that it shall not, by God! Melancholy faces like yours must be cheered up, and my dreary earnest I will keep to myself. My journey from Regensburg was devilish tiresome, and I missed you very much in that arch-catholic country. I am not fond of giving descriptions of journeys, least of all such as remind you of unpleasant feelings. May it suffice to say that I thought of you most affectionately, and that the image of the lovely Clara* stood before my eyes in waking and sleeping."

In this way the letter goes on, touching spasmodically upon friendship, Clara, money, or rather no money matters, and other heterogeneous subjects. I quote only one more passage: "At Bayreuth, I paid a visit to the widow of Jean Paul, who presented me with his portrait. I was introduced

---

* Not to be mistaken for that other "Clara," who was to become the faithful and congenial companion of Schumann. The lady here in question was a Miss Kurrer, whose acquaintance he made, when she was already engaged to be married, which, however, did not prevent him from admiring her most fervently. The friendly acquiescence of the real lover shows clearly the innocently romantic character of the whole affair.

through the kindness of old Mrs. Rollwenzel.* If the whole world read Jean Paul it would certainly be better, but also more unhappy. He has often brought me to the verge of madness, but the rainbow of peace always flows softly over the tears, and the heart grows wonderfully elevated and transformed. . . . Farewell, and be happy. May the genius of mankind be with thee, and that of joyful tears accompany thee for ever."

This short utterance must suffice us as a specimen of the general condition of Schumann's mind during his first sojourn at Leipsic. His way of life seems to have been of an isolated kind, at least as far as his fellow-students were concerned. The uncouth, mock enthusiasm of the so-called old Teutonic patriots, then in vogue at most of the German universities, could not but have a marring, inharmonious effect on the tender strings of his heart. As to his professional studies, there was a total absence of even an attempted beginning. A long time after his matriculation at the university, he writes to the above-mentioned

* The keeper of an inn near Bayreuth, which had become celebrated by several of Richter's works being written there.

friend: "I have not been to a single lecture, but have worked a good deal quietly, *i.e.* I have played the piano and written some Jean Pauliads."

As the most important event, both for his life and artistic career, we have now to consider the acquaintance with Friedrich Wieck and his daughter Clara, which Schumann made about this time. He took at once a great interest in the talented girl, who at the age of nine already grappled successfully with the technical difficulties of her instrument. Clara Wieck was a pupil of her father's, and of him now Schumann also took some pianoforte lessons, the first regular instruction he had had. In this favourable atmosphere his resolution of giving himself wholly to art grew more and more decided. In the meantime, however, the prejudices of his mother had to be considered, at least outwardly, and in order to satisfy her, Schumann left Leipsic for Heidelberg, where at that time the great legal authority Thibaut attracted a great many students. Unfortunately, or fortunately, the same professor took a most lively interest in music (witness his book about the ' Purity of Musical Art '), and the reader will easily guess which part of his master's knowledge had the greatest charm for our *soi-disant* law-student. Upon the whole, the year he stayed at Heidelberg seems to have been the happiest of Schumann's life, and one would fain dwell on this bright point of a career soon to be overshadowed by sorrow.

Art had now engrossed the whole essence of his being, and the technical study of his particular instrument was taken up by him with an enthusiastic spirit. Whole days were spent in practising on the piano, and even on his frequent excursions into the beautiful surroundings of Heidelberg, Schumann was never without a dumb keyboard, on which his fingers performed the most difficult passages, while the carriage of the friends was rolling along the smooth pavement of the Bergstrasse, or by the side of the Neckar.

It was also from Heidelberg that he entered for the first and last time the "land of song." From his trip to the north of Italy we possess two or three letters, which show the deep impression of southern nature and life on Schumann's susceptible heart. The "Jean Paulism" of former times reappears here in a more individualised, and in consequence less affected form, and at the same time we notice a descriptive power of considerable range and originality. We also hear of a quarrel at a coffee-house, in which Schumann behaved with great tact and spirit. The affair might have been of serious consequences, if his adversary had not ultimately discovered himself as a commercial gentleman of Hebrew descent, who was but too happy to drop his chivalrous grandiloquence, as soon as matters began to look serious. A beautiful English lady, to whom Schumann lost his heart at first sight, and who, parting from him at Venice, presented him sentimentally with a branch of cypress, may form the final tableau of this happy time of youthful freedom and enthusiasm.

On returning to Heidelberg, he had at once to face again the flood of troublesome realities. First of all a number of importunate creditors had to be quieted, and it was no easy task to make a conscientious guardian dole out a further allowance to his extravagant ward. The usual time for university studies had also nearly elapsed, and a legal examination was threatening, which Schumann felt himself wholly incapable of going through. At last he had to rally his spirits, and make a full confession of his doings to his mother. The letter in which this was done is still extant, and deserves a short notice on our part, as strongly indicative of our hero's characteristic shyness of utterance, which in this case was still increased by the tender consideration for his mother's well-known feelings, and which could be got over only by the firm persuasion, that the gain or loss of all his ideal goods was at stake.

At first he does not like to broach the subject: "Good morning, mamma," he slyly begins; "how shall I describe to you the bliss of this moment? The flame of spirits of wine is flickering and tossing against my coffee-machine, and the sky is pure and golden—one would like to kiss it. The whole spirit of the morning penetrates me fresh and sober. In addition, your letter is lying before me, in which a whole treasury of sentiment, wisdom, and virtue is discovered. My cigar is also excellent—in short, the world is sometimes very beautiful, *i.e.* man, if he would only rise early every morning." But this matutinal effusion is soon changed for a different tone. He begins to describe, in a most impressive manner, the struggle pervading his whole life between poetry and prose, "or will you call it *jus* and music;" he enters into, and tries to dispel, all his mother's prejudices against music as a profession, while on the other hand he points out the drawbacks of a legal career for a commoner, without great property or connections, and without real interest in lawyers' "miserable pennysquabbles." At last Friedrich Wieck is referred to as the best judge of his (Schumann's) musical talent, and to the decision of this umpire he promises to submit the final choice of a vocation.

The immediate result of this letter was another one from Mrs. Schumann to old Wieck, full of doubtful spelling and words underlined four or five times, in which the frightened mother implores the master not to be biassed by his own love of music to decide in accordance with Robert's wishes. This application, however, proved of no avail. Wieck had distinctly recognised the spark of genius in his pupil, and his decision was given accordingly. Soon afterwards Schumann returned to Leipsic, in order to complete his preparatory technical studies before appearing in public as a pianist.

The second and third decades of the present century were the halcyon days of the executive musician. Glory and riches poured down in an almost inexhaustible stream on the head of the fortunate *virtuoso*.

In reading of the enormous sums gained by Paganini, or of the ladies dividing the atomic remains of a cushion on which Franz Liszt had been sitting, one does not quite understand the anxiety of Mrs. Schumann in preventing her son from taking his share of this golden harvest, which his eminent talent seemed to secure him beyond doubt. About the ideal danger threatening his artistic individuality, and with it the progress of modern music, we may safely say she did not trouble herself. Whether her son would have been strong enough to withstand the alluring siren of ephemeral success, and follow the distant call of the true muse, is a difficult question to answer.

Luckily an accident, or shall we call it artistic Providence, saved him the trouble, with which a decision in favour of virtuous hardship against easy vice is only to be bought. In his eagerness to gain a perfectly even and independent action of each single finger on the piano, Schumann had invented a complicated machinery, by means of which, it seems, the third finger of his right hand was suspended, while the four others went through the most difficult evolutions. The consequence was that, after a little while, the sinew of the third finger was by unnatural extension weakened to such a degree, that it became all but disabled, and of course entirely unavailable for artistic purposes. This implied practically the loss of the whole right hand, and every thought of a career as an executive artist had forthwith to be relinquished. The pianoforte had lost one of its ablest representatives, but the gain of music as a whole was incommensurably greater.

2.

The first favourable result of Schumann's changed prospects, was the serious commencement of theoretical studies, against which he had felt till then a strong aversion. The influence which the late attainment of this fundamental part of music had on his compositions we shall have to consider before long. But first we must now turn to an event which for the following years was to lead the whole power of his mind into a different channel. This is the starting of a new musical journal, which, under the title *Neue Zeitschrift für Musik*, was soon to become the intellectual centre and mouthpiece of a new phase in the art of sound.

The circumstances under which this remarkable birth took place are described by the father, or to speak more accurately, one of the fathers, that is our composer, in the following manner:—" At the end of 1833 there met at Leipsic every evening a number of for the greater part young musicians, principally with a view to friendly intercourse, but also in order to exchange their thoughts about the art which had become the bread and wine of their life, *i.e.* music. It cannot be said that the musical conditions of Germany were at that time of a very satisfactory nature. On the stage Rossini wielded the sceptre, while the piano was almost exclusively dominated by Herz and Hünten. And nevertheless only a few years were passed, since Beethoven, Weber, and Schubert lived amongst us. It is true that Mendelssohn's star was rising, and of Chopin the Pole wonderful things were rumoured; but the lasting effect of these two came later. One day the idea struck the young enthusiasts, 'Let us not be idle lookers on, let us work in order that things may grow different and better, that the *poetry of art* may again receive its due honour!' In this way the first pages of a new 'Journal for Music' saw the light."

To the description of musical barrenness given by Schumann in the above we must add, that the only critical organ of consequence was the celebrated 'Musical Gazette'(Allgemeine musikalische Zeitung), which, edited by one Fink, still enjoyed to a great extent the prestige of critical infallibility attached to Rochlitz's name, and, true to its old traditions smiled down upon contemporary labour with a sublime ignorance, equalled only by its natural compound, impertinent self-assertion. To break the spell of this monstrous imposition was one of the chief aims of the "young musicians," and foremost of Schumann himself; and the achievement of his noble efforts, in counteracting the antiquated prejudices of Philistinism would alone secure him a prominent position amongst his fellow-workers in the domain of artistic progress.

From this, however, it must not be concluded that Schumann's writings bore any signs of that harsh and combative nature, which seems to be the character of all great reformers from Luther and Knox to Wagner. Schumann is, on the contrary, of a decidedly affirmative nature. We find in him only few traces of all-denying satire, or of the sublime indignation of genius against mediocrity. It seems, as if

P

he proceeded in his writings on the principle, that a single talent of tender nature, crushed by adverse criticism would be an absolute loss of greater consequence, than the harm that might possibly arise from a temporary success of well-intentioned inability. His accusations are therefore more directed against bad principles, like empty virtuosity, and similar vices, than against individual evil-doers. The only eminent men whom he has treated, with decided, nay harsh antagonism are, to the best of my knowledge, Meyerbeer and Richard Wagner. The spectacular attempts at clumsiest music-hall popularity, mixed up in the works of the first-mentioned composer with beauties of a high order, make it easy to account for the sweeping criticism of a sensitive nature like Schumann's; and as to his aversion to the works of by far the greatest creative power of the age, we shall also not be at a loss to find a psychological explanation of a phenomenon so astonishing at first sight.

On the other hand, the merits of the new critical organ in encouraging and introducing to the public notice a number of aspiring talents are undeniable. The very first appearance of Schumann in the journalistic career, even before his own paper was started, consisted in a panegyric of Chopin, whose " Opus II." had, after many previous unsuccessful attempts, just then found a publisher. Berlioz, the eccentric apostle of French romanticism in music, was first acknowledged and defended against the attacks of German pseudo-patriotism by Schumann, who did the same service to the talented young Englishman, William Sterndale Bennett.

The greatest praise is also due to Schumann's noble exertions in bringing to the light of public admiration the hidden treasures of Schubert's posthumous compositions. As a rule the world looks with a not unjustified suspicion on the discoveries of outsiders, from the artistic bequests of departed celebrities. Such men generally know best what may be conducive to their own greatness, and the non-publication of a work during their lifetime would in most cases not reflect favourably on the probability of its intrinsic value; barring of course reasons of personal discretion, which seldom or never apply to the inoffensive sphere of our art. The publication of some of Mendelssohn's *œuvres posthumes* for instance, shows distinctly the superiority of the master's own criticism over that of his ill-advised admirers.

But in Schubert's case this was different. With him the publication of a work was not a question of being willing, but of being able. We have mentioned in our last chapter, with how much hesitation even his works of smallest size and greatest popularity, that is his songs, were received by blockheaded publishers, who would have stood aghast at the offer of a symphony or opera, in which risk and chance would of course have been at still less favourable odds. Schubert's MS. scores were therefore treated at his death with a neglect quite in accordance with their low price in the market, and the search for them could not but highly attract the curiosity of a musical enthusiast.

When Schumann went to Vienna in 1838, his first pilgrimage was directed to the Währing cemetery, to offer his pious gift of flowers on the graves of Beethoven and Schubert. On that of the greater master he found a bush of wild roses, while Schubert's resting-place was unadorned. On Beethoven's tombstone he also discovered a steel pen which he preserved as a hallowed treasure, and ever afterwards only used to indite his most inspired thoughts. When Schumann left the graves, almost envying the one resting between such two, he was suddenly reminded of Schubert's surviving brother Ferdinand, and to his humble dwelling in a suburb of Vienna, he forthwith wended his way. "He knew me" Schumann says "from my admiration for his brother, as I had expressed it in public, and told and showed me many things. At last he let me look at the treasures of Franz Schubert's compositions, which he still possesses. The wealth, that lay heaped up, made me shudder with joy: what to take first, where to cease? Amongst other things, he also showed me the scores of several symphonies of which many had never been heard, while others had been tried, but put back again on the ground of their being too difficult and bombastic." One of those symphonies, that in C major, the largest and grandest in conception, Schumann chose and sent to Leipsic, where it soon afterwards was performed at a Gewandhausconcert under Mendelssohn's direction. The success was immediate and of deep import. Here the astonished world witnessed for the first time the powers, in a more expanded sphere, of a composer the very beauties of whose songs had hitherto proved fatal to his general fame.*

For Schumann this public sanction of his bold prognostication must have been a source of purest unselfish joy.

It remains to add a few remarks about the attitude of our critic towards his more successful rival Mendelssohn. It was that of unconditional admiration, sometimes bordering on the prostrate devotion of a worshipper. For more particular information about the relations of the two men, highly creditable as they are to the noble unselfishness of Schumann's mind, if not to his critical acumen, we refer the reader to his writings, collected and edited by himself, in four volumes, and also to the valuable work on his life, by Herr von Wasielewski.† I will only quote a

* The other symphonies alluded to (eight in number, some of them only partly finished) have since been obtained and produced at the Crystal Palace through the unceasing energy of Mr. G. Grove. This gentleman and Mr. A. Manns share with Schumann and Liszt the honour of having recognised, and made others recognise, the great beauties of Franz Schubert's instrumental compositions.

† It has been noticed, that in the collection of Mendelssohn's letters the name of Schumann occurs, if at all, only in an occasional manner. Considering the friendly intercourse in which

few sentences from a letter hitherto unpublished in Germany, which was addressed to a zealous contributor of the 'Neue Zeitschrift,' Herr von Zuccalmaglio. After his death it came, with sixteen others, into the possession of the present writer, and was published by him in the 'Academy.'* The reader may consider it, at the same time, as a specimen of Schumann's epistolary style at this period, and compare its milder enthusiasm with the unalloyed "Jean Paulism" of the young student. The date of the letter is Leipsic, January 31st, 1837, and, as the only commentary required, I will add, that "Erste Töne," was an article on Mendelssohn, which had appeared in Schumann's paper, and that Wedel was one of Zuccalmaglio's numerous pseudonyms:

both stood at Leipsic, it is almost incredible that Mendelssohn should in his remarks on music have wholly ignored the numerous and, at any rate, original works of his admiring friend. The circumstance is generally explained from a narrow-minded jealousy of the editors of Mendelssohn's Letters, who might not be desirous of adding his testimonial to the rival composer's overpowering fame; but would it not be also possible to conjecture, that the admiration of the two masters was not mutual, and that Mendelssohn's utterances have been wisely suppressed, as not redounding to the credit of his liberal-mindedness?

* See Appendix II.

"My dear Sir,

"First of all I must tell you, how I gave Mendelssohn, with whom I dine every day, your article, 'Erste Töne.' I stood aside and watched his face to see what impression would be made upon him by your last sentence, which, I confess, had several times brought the tears into my own eyes. He read the article attentively; his face (what a glorious, divine face it is!) revealed all his impressions as he came to the passage. It was a pity you could not see him. 'Ha!' he cried, 'what's this? That is really too much: I am quite delighted. There are different kinds of praise; but this comes from a pure heart.' You should have seen him and heard him. 'Ten thousand thanks to the man who wrote this.' So he went on until we dived into our champagne. The fact is, as I have long ago made up my mind, there is no man who can write on music like Wedel; and I think I can read the same verdict in the delicate but continued motion of Mendelssohn's countenance, which is a record of all that is passing both within and without him. . . . . Do you know his *St. Paul*, in which one beauty relieves another without interruption? He was the first to grant to the Graces a place in the house of God, where they certainly ought not to be forgotten. Hitherto they have not been able to make their voices heard for the multitude of fugues. Do read *St. Paul*—the sooner the better. You will find in it nothing of Handel or Bach, whatever people may say, except in so far as all church music must be alike,'" etc.

Thus much about Schumann's critical power. Upon the whole it must be said that his influence on the progress of contemporary music was of a beneficial kind. Young aspiring talents were sure to find friendly appreciation, and in many cases, valuable advice, in the columns of the new organ, from which, on the other hand, the currents of vulgar puff were strictly excluded. Schumann had the instinctive horror of a gentleman against the low practices of artistic humbug, and sometimes, as in the case of Meyerbeer, was not able to perceive the good crop in the midst of luxuriant weeds. It must also be confessed that chiefly in his latter years he was by no means free from that onesidedness, inseparable as it seems from creative genius, which looks upon everything outside of its own circle of light as utter darkness.

It remains to say a few words about the style in which the results of Schumann's speculative power were delivered, which was a very extraordinary one indeed. Here are some extracts from a *soi-disant* criticism on Chopin's *Don Juan* fantasia, which was published by Schumann in the old 'Musical Gazette,' two years before the starting of his own journal. One can imagine the astonishment of the faithful reader of this solemn organ, when, amongst the utterances of his Dryasdust oracle, he suddenly hit upon the following eccentric effusion: "An Opus II.—Eusebius gently opened the door. You know the ironical smile on his pale face, which he puts on to make one curious. I was sitting at the piano with Florestan. Florestan, as you know, is one of those rare music-individuals who divine everything, future, new and extraordinary in advance. Still to-day he was to be taken by surprise. Eusebius called out: 'Hats off, gentlemen, here goes a genius,' and opened a piece of music before us. The title we were not allowed to see. I was glancing through the book half unconsciously; this veiled enjoyment of music without sound has a particular charm for me. Besides, it seems to me as if each single composer had his own groupings of notes for the eye. Beethoven looks different on paper from Mozart, in the same way as the prose of Jean Paul looks unlike that of Goethe. But now it was to me as if numbers of strange eyes were strangely looking at me, eyes of flowers, of basilisks, of butterflies, of girls. At other places it became lighter; I thought I heard Mozart's *La ci darem* winding through hundreds of harmonies; Leporello seemed to wink, and Don Juan flew past me in his white cloak."

The article goes on, describing in the same exalted strain, how the young enthusiasts play the piece with increasing delight, which is brought to a climax of admiring bewilderment when they find, on referring to the title-page, that the work is not by Beethoven or Schubert, but an Opus II., a *début* of an unknown composer, Frédéric Chopin. They forthwith repair to their adviser and friend, Master Raro, who smiles at their new idol with the cautious wisdom of his riper years, but promises a close scrutiny of the case. The final scene shows Florestan reclining on his sofa in a half dream, expounding the poetical inspirations found by him in Chopin's "Variations," intermixed with sundry remarks of a more critical character on the structure of the new piece.

I have on purpose quoted from the first article ever produced by Schumann, because, although in a slightly exaggerated form, it fully shows at once the power and weakness of his æsthetic writings. He never attempted to give an objective, or, as it is more grandly but less correctly called, an *impartial* analysis of a composition. He felt himself that the position of one creative mind towards another must have a strong alloy of personal bias in it. This he never even tries to conceal, and for that very reason he personifies the various sides of his own character, and shows how differently one and the same work may have acted upon him in different moods, or might act according to the predisposition of the mind to which it appealed. Florestan and Eusebius, who have been introduced to the reader in the foregoing sketch, are only, to speak with Faust, the "two souls in his breast;" Eusebius the mild receptive dreamer, Florestan the fiery enthusiast, wild and impulsive in his hatred and love, and armed with a divine recklessness with regard to other people's prejudices.

These two are stereotyped figures in Schumann's writings. His articles are alternately signed with either pseudonym, according to the tone of their criticism. Sometimes they both give their individual judgments on one and the same work, and in such cases Master Raro (also known to the reader), who was meant to symbolise the calmly speculative side in Schumann's nature, is referred to for final judgment. Sometimes also various other characters, like Julius and Zelia, are introduced and grouped together in a kind of brotherhood or secret society —"more than secret," as Schumann himself afterwards declared, "for it existed only in the head of its founder." The name of this imaginary society was the "Davidsbund," probably from King David and his celebrated harp. At one time, however, it does not seem to have been quite as imaginary, as might be concluded from the just quoted lines, which, by the way, were written nearly twenty years later, and at a period when Schumann looked back upon the eccentricities of his youth from a distance greater even than that marked by this lapse of time. Raro was generally considered to have been the personification of Friedrich Wieck, and certain features of other David-associates were also traced to persons of real existence.

How seriously the plan of an actual society (perhaps somewhat analogous to the "Pre-Raphaelite brotherhood" in this country) was considered by Schumann, becomes for the first time evident from a passage in the once before cited series of letters. "I have a variety of plans and schemes for which I want your assistance," writes Schumann to Zuccalmaglio on May 18th, 1837. "First of all I have been thinking for a long time of giving real life to the Davidsbund, by bringing men of the same opinion (even if not professional musicians) in a closer connection by means of *signs* and *symbols*.

If academics with dunces at their heads, designate their members, why should not we, the younger generation, do the same?" Although this scheme of an academy with anti-academicians as members proved abortive, the charm of Florestan and Eusebius as imaginary creations remains unimpaired, and it is with regret that the reader of Schumann's collected works sees them turn up more and more seldom, till at last they quite disappear, together with a good deal of their originator's freshness of style and perception. The fact is that in his later years Schumann's position in musical questions became essentially altered, and he used against himself that sweeping judgment, which in the inarticulate longings of his early career could only see the juvenile and silly. Unfortunately the same remark applies to his views about the ultimate aims of his art, and the breakage which we discern in the development of his æsthetical notions could not but react upon the direction of his creative power.

The deeper causes of the vital change in the whole artistic existence of Schumann, which after a gradual growth of many years reached its climax with the beginning of his third or "orchestral" period, we shall have to consider in the ensuing remarks.

3.

In the first chapter of this book I have tried to follow as closely as possible the rise of what I called the "poetic principle in music" from the earliest times till Beethoven. I have shown that in every art there exists a duality of intention, namely, on one side the original passionate impulse, previous to its taking any distinct form, and secondly, the innate order of beauty belonging to the particular art in question. I further tried to prove that the intensity of this impulse in Beethoven's later works all but broke through the forms of music proper, and at last, in the Ninth Symphony, absolutely required the complement of words. The consistent carrying out of Beethoven's grand reformatory act, I at last professed to see in Wagner's music-drama.

Schumann also felt instinctively the necessity of introducing the fresh life of poetical pulsation into the dead formalism of absolute music. We have seen before that he wrote on his banner the war cry of "poetry in art," and that he acknowledges the affinity between his art and contemporary phases of literature, by calling himself and his friends *romantic* musicians. The works of his first period, all conceived at and written for the pianoforte, show in their small forms all that pointedness of exaggerated, not to say transcendental, sentimentalism which forms the typical character of Richter's prose, and (mixed up already with self-consuming irony) of Heine's lyrics. It seems, indeed, as if the demand of some connection with the art of poetry had been felt at that time by musicians of the most divergent tendencies. Even Mendelssohn acknowledged it in a certain sense by calling his short pianoforte pieces "songs without words;" that is, snatches of lyrical effusion, with an underlying although not expressed poetical meaning. On the other hand, it is well known how the occult idea struggling in Beethoven's later works ran riot in the mind of the young medical student Berlioz. With the strong aversion of the French character against purely ideal generalisations, he looked for a more tangible basis of his inspiration, and in consequence clad the lofty conceptions of Beethoven in the distinct forms of a story.

Schumann, as we have seen, declared himself the advocate of Berlioz, whom he imitated to a certain extent by affixing to his lyrical pianoforte pieces titles sometimes full of poetic suggestiveness, but not seldom also without any recognisable relation to the character of the piece. But, strange to say, Schumann always laid particular stress upon the fact, that these denominations had been added to the composition after its being finished, with a view only to guiding the player, as to the way in which it was to be rendered. This one fact is sufficient to show the utter misconception on the part of Schumann of Beethoven's reformatory efforts. For it proves that the expression of a distinct poetic idea, as we discerned it in Beethoven, was at all times absent from his mind. In reality, the music even of his 'Sturm und Drang' period was quite as absolute as that of Mozart and Haydn. The poetic element in his works never amounted to more than the unconscious mood in which every work of art must be conceived, but never passed through the medium of conscious feeling before its embodiment in sound. To say that in the 'Carnival' or the 'Papillons' the pure source of Beethoven's mighty tradition is flowing, and to invest the slender form of the most subjective lyrist with the grand folds of the prophet's cloak, seems indeed almost too absurd even for the blindest worshipper. Still, such is the hue and cry of a powerful school in music called after our composer's name, and represented by an imposing number of talented and devoted disciples. The fact, however, is, that to the master himself, as well as to his pupils, something in Beethoven has remained, and, as it seems, will remain for ever an indissoluble mystery. The numerous attempts of Schumann to bring down Beethoven's grand conceptions to the level of his own whimsical romanticism, sometimes result in the most glaring incongruities. In the wonderful Finale of Beethoven's Symphony in A major, he sees only the description of a jolly wedding, the bride being "a celestial maiden with a rose in her hair, but one only," etc. etc. In comparing this *jargon* of sentimental affectation with the programme to the Ninth Symphony, written by Wagner more than five and twenty years ago,* one can indeed not remain doubtful, in which of the two composers' works to look for the continued flow of the great master's inspiration.

In thinking it my duty to oppose current prejudices, it is at the same time far from my wish to deny the indescribable beauty of Schumann's early works, which bear undoubtedly the stamp of genius of the first order. All the charms of indistinct longing, of

* See Appendix, page 292.

youthful enthusiasm, and of the most striking originality in conception and execution, fill us with ever fresh delight in listening to the strains of the Sonata in F sharp minor, the Études Symphoniques, or the Kreisleriana; and upon the occasional eccentricities or shortcomings in their formal treatment, we are inclined to look with a much less critical eye than the composer himself used to do at a later period.

We have recognised a strong desire on Schumann's part of embodying his individual feelings and sufferings in his art, a desire for which the pianoforte alone, even with the enlarged scope opened to it by his own works, could scarcely be considered as the appropriate instrument. Schumann also felt the want of the spoken word as the firm starting-point of his lofty flights, and he was fortunate enough to find a poet full of the deepest pathos, and at the same time congenial to himself by the strongly individualised mode of his expression. This poet was Heinrich Heine, the "spoiled favourite of the graces," the hero and victim of modern thought and misery, "the knight with the laughing tear in his scutcheon," who descended into the deepest depths of the heart, and brought back the jewels of his songs, clear and flashing like ice, but reflecting in their crystalline surface the brightest rays and the darkest shades of human passion.

And here again I am sorely tempted to digress upon a subject nearest to my interest, viz. the almost total absence of what might be called "artistic song" in the literature of this island, the causes of which I find partly in the disdain of poets to stoop to the simple utterance of the popular muse, partly in the particular nature of this popular poetry itself, which to a prevailing extent took the narrative form of the ballad, and therefore seemed less adapted for the infusion of lyrical impulse.*

* I must add here, parenthetically, that the charming snatches of song of disputed origin, transmitted to us in Elizabethan dramas, seem to me to show distinctly the traces of artistic consciousness, and are indeed partly referable to professional poets, like 'Come with me, and be my love,' to Kit Marlowe. They, therefore, do not quite come under the category of popular song, and show indeed but slight affinity with the 'Volkslied.' Robert Burns, on the other hand, the great singer of songs, purposely limited himself to the simplicity of popular feeling, and, therefore, although a great artist, did not write what I have called "artistic songs" *par excellence.* I will, however, by no means deny that the songs of both Burns and the Elizabethan poets, and the remnants of the old tunes to which most of them were written,

Or was it perhaps the want of music as a national art, which failed to encourage the great English lyrists to proportionate efforts in this direction, and induced, for instance, Byron to assign always his weakest stanzas "to music?" But I feel but too deeply how abrupt and "not proven" my remarks in their necessary conciseness must appear, and therefore gladly return to my immediate subject.

The high position which Schumann takes among the masters of German song, has been sufficiently defined by his being called the musical exponent of Heine. It seems, indeed, not unlikely that the verdict of an impartial posterity will base his chief claims to immortality on such works as the settings of 'Ich grolle nicht,' and the whole 'Dichterliebe' series, not to speak of innumerable other 'Lieder,' small in form, but contain hopeful germs of the regeneration of English lyrical music on a national basis. I have myself, on another occasion, expressed my belief in this desired possibility by word and deed. Only we must first of all clear the English song, on the one hand, from the atmosphere of the music-hall attaching to it, and on the other, from the strong tinge of sentimental Philistinism which, in my eyes, is one of the most dangerous vices of this nation, fostered in our particular case by the overpowering influence of Mendelssohn and his imitators.

disclosing the infinite perspective of lyrical pathos, and unsurpassable in the congenial rendering of the poet's sentiments. It is true that Schumann did not invent or even advance the artistic form of the song. This form indeed occurs with its essential variations in Beethoven himself, and was after him filled with the inexhaustible beauties of Schubert's melodiousness. But Beethoven's broad dramatic conceptions were always to some extent embarrassed by the narrow limits of the song, and in Schubert we miss sometimes that careful entering into the minutest intentions of the poet, which must be considered as the prominent feature of the latest phase of music. Besides, both these great composers were extremely limited as to the poetical materials at their disposal. The artistic song in German literature dates only from Goethe, and his acquaintance with Herder's researches in international popular poetry. Goethe remained the only valuable resort of Beethoven's, and for a long time also of Schubert's lyrical muse. The latter master only recognised the rising stars of Heine and Rükert. Schumann's position in this respect was much more favoured by fortune. He stood in the midst of the literary movement of his time, and was prepared both by his genius and education to recast the newly acquired treasures of poetry in the mould of his own art. The progress, therefore, marked by his songs was achieved by poetical rather than by musical means, another proof of the organic and indivisible connection of the two sister arts.

The duration of Schumann's song-time was comparatively short. The greater part of his *Lieder* were written in 1840, a year which, at the same time, was the most eventful in his quiet life. The rest of the working time allotted to him—for he did work to the last incessantly—was given up to the greater forms of vocal and instrumental music, as the oratorio, symphony, and the various kinds of chamber music. This third period might be briefly characterised as the *return to form*. We have mentioned the strong aversion which Schumann at first felt for the serious study of the technical basis of his art. The contempt against the established rules, as witnessed in his juvenile works, although to a great extent arising from the boldness of aspiring genius, was also partly due to his actual want of fundamental knowledge, and this neglect could not but result in a strong reaction as the composer reached the stage of artistic discretion. He now became a fervent advocate of the necessity and venerableness of established rules, and conscientiously removed the traces of his youthful eccentricities from revised editions of his earlier works. It is also from this point of view that we must judge the objections raised by him against the gigantic attempts at revolutionising and reconstructing musical art from top to bottom, which have made the name of Richard Wagner the symbol of hope for the rising generation. Or was it perhaps the instinctive aversion of the failing against the successful man, which, added to the entirely heterogeneous nature of Wagner's genius, in this one instance overcame the usual generosity of Schumann's character, and made his own war cry of "poetry in music" sound harsh and dreadful from his rival's lips?

The works of Schuman's third period are numerous and comprise almost all the forms of vocal and instrumental music, not always treated with equal success, but always full of power, and of that strong touch of individuality which forms a prominent feature of his nature. We count among these, four symphonies, with the fragments of a fifth, two so-called profane oratorios, the 'Peri,' after Moore's well-known poem from 'Lalla Rookh,' and the 'Pilgrimage of the Rose,' both full of lyrical and phantastic beauties of the first order, but lagging occasionally through an evident want of dramatic concentration, combined with a tendency towards painting in detail. The same want of the broad conception of a dramatic poet proved absolutely fatal to his only opera, *Genevieve*, which, notwithstanding the redeeming charms of numerous beautiful passages, has never been able to move the hearts of the hearers with the irresistible force of dramatic passion.

It is also a noticeable fact that the two representative heroes of modern thought and doubt, 'Manfred' and 'Faust,' have been favoured subjects of Schumann's muse. The spark of 'Weltschmerz' (as the Germans call the spirit of deepest despondency and fierce defiance, resulting from the wisdom of our latter days) in Byron's poem, was sufficient to kindle the congenial flame in the composer's bosom, and inspire him with conceptions never surpassed in depth of pathos, and bitterness of self-torturing passion. The setting, on the other hand, of the epilogue in heaven of Goethe's *Faust* displays the rest after life's battle of which the longing soul dreams in its purest aspirations, and ranks with its deep *chiaroscuro* of mystical ecstasy amongst the highest efforts which our art has ever been capable of.

It would be exceeding the original plan of this book merely to hint at the numerous interesting points of discussion suggested by the latter part of Schumann's career. Our purpose was chiefly to show the true character of the progressive side of his activity, falsely connected with Beethoven's latest works, with which in reality it shows only a slight resemblance. This revolutionary spirit was, the contrary, to repeat it again, disavowed by the work of Schumann's riper years. The contempt of form coincided in him, with his ignorance of it; when he began to master the technical part of his art, he clung to it with unflinching fidelity. Considering him merely as a reformer of music on a poetical basis, as his *quand même* admirers are but too inclined to do, we should have to call his career a decided failure, if it did not seem altogether ungrateful to mention such a word in connection with a man who has given us the 'Carnival,' the Songs, 'Faust,' and the Symphony in C.

4.

We have only a few words to add about Schumann's personal character, and the events which form the scanty materials for his biography.

Even in the buoyancy of youthful enthusiasm, he was distinguished by a particular kind of apparent absent-mindedness, which, without preventing his listening attentively to what was going on, still would not let him take an active part in the conversation. His increasing silence became proverbial among his friends. Once, it is told, he entered a lady's drawing-room, smiled in his placid way at the company present, and opening the piano, played a few chords; after which he made his exit, smiling again, but without having spoken a single syllable. Only on rare occasions, and amongst very intimate friends, an interesting topic would induce him to give full utterance to his opinions. The characteristic feature of his personal existence was an utter want of demonstrativeness, sometimes amounting to actual shyness. Schumann himself was conscious of this fact, and has described his social accomplishments with the almost exaggerated modesty characterising also his numerous sayings about his own art. "I shall be very glad to see you here," he writes to Zuccalmaglio. "In me, however, you must not expect to find much. I scarcely ever speak except in the evening, and most in playing the piano."

His professional career may be summed up in the fewest words. After editing his musical journal for nearly ten years, he went to Dresden, with no particular position,' but that of conductor of a singing academy. From there he was called to Düsseldorf, in order to lead the concerts of the celebrated musical institute of that city. His official duties, however, proved soon too much for his declining health; and after a few years he dropped the baton for ever, without great loss to art or to himself, nature having refused him the most essential qualities of a conductor. The monotony of his daily life was occasionally interrupted by artistic tours, amongst which those to Russia and Holland were the most successful. On both occasions he was accompanied by his wife, the celebrated *pianiste*, Clara Schumann, so well known as the congenial interpreter of her husband's inspirations, both on the Continent and in England. The union with her was the source of deepest happiness to him. Won after many troubles, and against the obstinate resistance of her father, Friedrich Wieck, she remained Schumann's truest friend and helpmate, affianced to him not only by the power of love, but also by the elective bonds of genius. It has seldom been the happy lot of an artist to see his most intimate feelings and aspirations so perfectly understood, nay even interpreted to the world, by the mother of his children.

But even this faithful companion could not ward off his doom. As early as 1833, Schumann's friends were frightened by a state of morbidness in his feelings, which, increased by the sudden news of a near relation's death, at last led to an attack of what seems to have been very like actual madness. He himself speaks in his diary of "the dreadful night of the 17th of October," and a clue to this mysterious expression we may see in the circumstance that he immediately changed the fourth story in which he was living at the time for a lower one, and never afterwards could be induced to take up his quarters in the upper part of a house. From that time the foreshadowed idea of his fate seems never to have been absent from his mind, showing itself in an unaccountable horror of anything connected with madness. So when the position at Düsseldorf is first offered to him, he writes to Hiller for advice as though on a point of vital importance: "I was looking the other day in an old geographical book for information about Düsseldorf, and there I found mentioned, amongst the curiosities, three nunneries and one lunatic asylum. Against the former I have not the slightest objection, but about the latter it was very unpleasant to me to read."

I will not trouble the reader with a detailed account of the slow progress of the terrible fate which was to extinguish the flame of Schumann's genius. The following passage from a letter may suffice to indicate the circumstances which contributed to hasten the catastrophe. It shows at the same time how, even in the wildest flights of his troubled imagination, the absorbing interest of his mind remained his art. The letter from which we quote is addressed to Hiller, and dated—

Düsseldorf, April 23, 1853.

"Yesterday we have been rapping tables for the first time. It is a wonderful power. Fancy, I asked it about the rhythm of the two first bars of the symphony in C minor. At first it refused to answer; but at last it began, ♩♪♪♪|♩||, but very slowly. When I told it, 'But this is much too slow, my dear table,' it began at once beating the right time. I also asked, if it could tell me the number I was thinking of, and it answered correctly, 'Three.' We were all of us in utter amazement, and felt surrounded with miracles. Enough, I was to-day too full of what I had seen not to speak of it."

According to a tradition, Beethoven, when asked about the poetic meaning of the mentioned motive of his fifth symphony, answered: "So klopft das Schicksal an die Pforte" ("It is thus that destiny knocks at the gate"). For Schumann these words proved to contain a prophetic warning. Not quite a year after the date of this letter he tried to drown the horrors of his approaching madness in the Rhine, and on the 20th of July, 1856, he died in the asylum at Endenich, near Bonn, in the cemetery of which town he lies buried.

CHAPTER IV.

ROBERT FRANZ AND FRANZ LISZT.

1.

IN the last two chapters we have witnessed the growth of German song from its simple germ of popular feeling into an organism of highly developed power and beauty. The seed of Schubert and Schumann had fallen on good soil. To Mendelssohn we owe a number of songs, equal in elegant finish to the other compositions of that master of form, and some of them full of deepest sentiment; and the laurels of this triad could not but cause sleepless nights of emulous desire to the smaller fry of contemporary musicians. What I said before about the apparent simplicity of the poetical form of the song, applies to a great extent also to its musical treatment. In consequence the musical market was soon swamped with a never ceasing flow of lyrical effusion, and the typical shibboleth of "Sechs Lieder für eine Singstimme" on the Opus 1 of aspiring youths became a sign of horror to the German critic.

But this loud chorus of babbling mediocrity must not deafen us to the voices of the prophets of true genius. Amongst the disciples of Schumann, for instance, we count men like Rubinstein, Brahms, J. O. Grimm, and others, with full sounding names in the land of song. Still, it cannot be said that these composers have essentially advanced the form of the song in the abstract. Brahms, for instance, where he tries to expand the limits of this form (in his 'Romanzen from Tieck's Schöne Magelone'), looses hold of the essential features of the species itself, that is, he writes beautiful pieces of vocal music of a nondescript character, and of no relevancy with regard to the formal, and still less to what we call the *poetical progress* of the song.

This takes us back to the starting point of our researches, *i.e.*, the victory of pure poetic impulse over musical formalism, the accomplishment of which we discerned in Wagner's music-drama.

R

The same process we now shall witness in a modified way in the latest phase of lyrical music. For this purpose I will introduce the reader to two living masters of song, both of strongly pronounced individuality, and neither of them under the direct influence of any of the above-mentioned writers. I am speaking of Franz Liszt and Robert Franz.

The artistic career of both has been widely different, and their treatment of the particular form of art in question has also little in common; still there is one feature peculiar to either, which is sufficiently important to explain the combination of their names in these pages, and indicative at the same time of the only basis on which a further organic progress of the song seems possible. Liszt and Franz are both *poets*, before they are *musicians*. The strength of their musical renderings depends entirely on the beauty of the words interpreted by them. In composers of the last century we often observe, how very little their music is connected with, and therefore depends upon, the underlying text, and even Schubert makes us forget occasionally the silliness of his words by dint of absolute melodious charm. But both Liszt and Franz are in an eminent sense masters of the modern, or shall we call it the "future" school. Their inspiration is essentially of a receptive, feminine kind, and the greater or less intrinsic value of a poem set by them may infallibly be guessed by perusing their music even without the words.

2.

In writing down the name of Robert Franz I am sadly conscious that to many of my English readers its characters may be an all but new or, at least, a most unwonted sight. His songs do not appear on the programmes of our numerous ballad concerts; indeed, I am not sure that many of them have been publicly sung in London, a fact which once more shows the sad deficiencies of mutual intercourse amongst the nations, even in that most international of languages, music. For in his own country, the place of Franz, amongst the greatest masters of song, and as the first of living lyrists is disputed by few, and in the concert-halls of Boston and New York his works are, it is said, received with enthusiasm; the question, why it should have been easier for the wings of his fame to cross the Atlantic, than the narrow strip of water to which England owes so much, deserves the grave consideration of the music publisher, the geographer, and the student of national phrenology. I myself feel but too deeply the great disadvantage of having to construct my conclusions on facts and premises unknown to the reader; but seeing that all exponents of new things are heirs to the same evil, I must strengthen my courage with the hope, that here and there some one may be induced by my words to test their veracity by personal investigation.*

The considerable amount of critical literature produced in Germany, *ad vocem* R. Franz, has, upon the whole, proved of little use in furthering my aims. The help for instance which the 'Study on Robert Franz,' by the well-known historian, W. Ambros, might possibly afford me, would be more than outweighed by the time and patience I should have to spend in pointing out, and eventually combating, shades of opinion more or less at variance with my

* Three selections of Franz's works, containing together more than a hundred songs, have been published by the firms of Leuckart, Peters, and Breitkopf und Härtel of Leipsic, and may be had for almost the same price as Englishmen are willing to pay for one or two commonplace ballads of native growth.

own. The only exception here forms Franz Liszt; the impressive eloquence of his style shows nowhere to greater advantage than in pleading the merits of men whom a nature less generous would look upon as dangerous rivals. I shall quote from the biographical part of his pamphlet on "Robert Franz," the more freely, as in this way my former remarks on the graceful elegance of Liszt's writings will best be illustrated. As a still more valuable clue to the hidden sources of our composer's inspiration, I have to mention several interesting letters addressed by him to me, the use of which, for my present purpose, has been kindly granted.

Robert Franz was born in 1815 at Halle, a small university town in Prussian Saxony. His early youth passed without any incidents of importance. The atmosphere in his father's house was that of old-fashioned narrowmindness, and when the first signs of musical talent showed themselves, the boy found no encouragement. Only reluctantly his father allowed him to profit by what little instruction the second-rate music teachers of his native town could afford. Even under the oppressive influence of four different masters Franz knew how to preserve intact the spontaneous freedom of his feeling. This state of self-asserted liberty, dangerous as it might have been to many, contributed, as Liszt remarks, perhaps more than anything else towards the autodidactic character of Franz's talent. "For the elect of the muse, the predestined of art, are like the bees which, from the petals of poisonous flowers, suck forth sweet aromatic nourishment." The desire of every true musician of executing and hearing himself execute, or, as Liszt puts it, his longing for virtuosity in some form, Franz satisfied by applying himself passionately to the organ. It is said that of a Sunday he used to race from one church to another, asking the various cantors to let him play part of the service. This extraordinary zeal was considered by his father and his masters at the college, as a mild form of lunacy, dangerous in so far only as it detained the youth from the more "solid" branches of learning; his co-disciples were apt to treat the silent and timid enthusiast as a downright fool.

Only the musical professor of the college recognised the gift of his pupil and raised him to the post of accompanist of the choir. It was here that he became acquainted with the works of Handel, Haydn, and Mozart, which fell like the first message of hope into the dark maze of his unguided ideas, confirming, at the same time, his resolution of becoming an artist himself. Under this influence Franz also ventured upon his own first creative attempts, without any systematic knowledge of theory; not unlike, in this respect, Wagner and Schumann, who both, about the same time, and separated by not many miles, were groping their various ways towards the distant ideal.

At last the growing love for art in Franz's bosom overcame his natural timidity and the filial affection to his well-meaning but prejudiced parents. He declared his unalterable desire of continuing his artistic studies under a master of his craft, and at last gained an unwilling consent from his father. The well-known composer Frederic Schneider, living at that time in the neighbouring Dessau, was chosen for this purpose, and to him Franz went full of hope, and thirsting for knowledge and encouragement.

This hope was to be disappointed. Schneider was a dry formalist, without sympathy for inspirations that could not be derived from, or measured by, the strict rules of counterpoint. It seems that among his own pupils there existed an opposition party, with independent notions about the aims of music, and nothing was more natural than that Franz should have joined this group of dissenting freethinkers, who used to hold secret meetings to exercise the divine art after their own fashion. Under the circumstances much good could not be expected from Schneider's instructions; and when, in 1837, after an absence of two years, Franz returned to his father's house, the results of his apprenticeship were not of a kind to reconcile his parents with his choice of vocation. It is true that he had amassed a considerable amount of theoretical knowledge, and could also show a corresponding heap of "original" productions, strongly flavoured with the dust of the schoolroom; but these were not of a kind to satisfy anybody but their author.

The question what to do next was approaching uncomfortably near. His reserved, aristocratic nature prevented Franz from pushing his own way by means of drawing-room coteries; on all sides he was discouraged and repelled; at last he himself began to lose the student's pride which at first had assisted him in bearing up against the tide of disappointment. A state of morbid despondency was the consequence, in which only the intuitive love and sympathy of his mother saved him from perishing.

About this period Franz began the serious study of the works of Sabastian Bach, and in the same degree as he entered into the mysterious depths of this grand master, he grew less and less satisfied with his own achievements. Here he found the climax of polyphonous art combined with, and made serviceable to, a breadth of conception to which the training of the schoolroom offered no clue. The voice of true human feeling spoke to his congenial spirit through the din of scholastic wisdom. At the same time the lyrical passion of Schubert, together with the movement of romanticism proclaimed by Schumann's compositions and critical writings, found an echo in Franz's bosom, imbuing him with the more rapid and impulsive passion of modern art.

The peculiar conditions of his genius are generally traced back to the influence of Handel and Bach on the one, and Schubert and Schumann on the other side, and it cannot be denied that the impressions received from these four masters' works during a stage of transition has been of considerable importance for his mode of thought and utterance. But there is distinguishable in his style a something which cannot be derived from either of the two elements just mentioned, and which, with Franz himself, we are inclined to look for in the old Lutheran choral which formed "the earliest and most lasting artistic impression" of his youth. Of this, more anon.

The process of assimilation of the classic and romantic elements occupied from five to six years. During this time Franz was also deeply interested in the progressive movement of German philosophy, which at that time found a local centre and an organ in the celebrated "Hallesche Jahrbücher," edited by the staunch Hegelian partisan, Arnold Ruge. All this while Franz refrained from artistic production, patiently waiting for the moment when, after the processes of fermenting and clearing being over, "he would have to say a word for himself." This time came at last not without a powerful impulse of personal feeling; "it coincided—to quote Liszt's eloquent words—with a moment of deep passion which, in shaking all the fibres of his soul, also moved the strings of poetic inspiration. He loved with a devotion as it can only bud in a pure and noble nature. He dreamt of happiness . . . . its wing touched him gently—then it fled. This catastrophe of his internal fate decided his artistic maturity." His production henceforth was fresh and spontaneous, for " he wrote in order to give an outlet to his overflowing sensations—*per sfogarsi.*"

The first effort of his muse showed a ripeness of feeling and technical skill rarely met with amongst beginners, but easily explained in this case from the composer's self-restraint for so many preceding years. I know indeed of no artist's works the grouping of which according to time or maturity, would present greater difficulties than the four hundred songs of Robert Franz; we may easily discern a considerable variety in the degree of their intrinsic value according to the greater or lesser happiness of momentary inspiration, but that progress through different stages of intellectual development, of which young artists are, alas, but too apt to make the public a witness, Franz has hidden entirely from the gazer's eye. His Opus 1 was accordingly treated with great respect by contemporary critics, and excited in particular the admiration of Robert Schumann, who himself introduced the new composer to the readers of his paper and otherwise assisted him with his usual kindness. Ever since, his fame has continued increasing gradually but uninterruptedly, and the acknowledgment of his talent abroad at last obliged even his fellow citizens to relent from their cold reserve towards the prophet in their midst. The distinctions of organist at one of the parish churches, and of conductor of the town concerts, were conferred upon him, and the university offered him a chair for music, which he occupies to the present day.

This is in bare outline the life of Robert Franz; somewhat monotonous and void of incident, but not without signs of mental strife and sorrow, of deeper import, perhaps, for the growth of lyrical faculties than the stirring passions of the great world. For who knows the laws after which the sensitive plant "opens its leaves to the light," or the hidden sources from which genius draws its nourishment? But let us now look at the flowers which sprang from the unbroken evenness of this soil.

3.

Robert Franz was from the beginning conscious of the strictly lyrical nature of his talent, and with a self-criticism rare among artists, he limited himself exclusively to his own sphere, without even attempting a flight into the regions of the more absolute forms of music. His works, amounting in all to forty-four, consist, with one or two exceptions only, of songs. But this self-chosen onesidedness is not in his case a sign of limited power. In the narrow space of the song he displays with more than ordinary skill the most intricate combinations of musical art, and even without his editorial labour the world might recognise in Franz the thorough student f Bach and Handel by the fine contrapuntal texture of his pianoforte accompaniments. In the instrumental parts of his songs, with the strict and independent guidance of their single voices, we also see clearly a strong influence of the Lutheran choral which, moreover, the composer himself is ready to acknowledge, and through which he traces his intimate connection with the *Volkslied*. It is this strictly polyphonous, not to say vocal character of his accompaniments, which distinguishes them essentially from those of other modern masters, and connects them with the treatment of the instruments in Bach and Handel.

The remarks on this point made by Franz himself, are of such interest and throw so new a light on an important side of musical history, that I feel sure the reader will be thankful for the following extracts from one of his letters.

"There is no doubt—Franz writes—that the basis of all musical forms is the vocal and not the instrumental style. The human voice existed previous to all instruments, the latter being indeed only a mechanical means of imitating the former. From the beginning of the fourteenth to the end of the eighteenth century we perceive an independent development of the vocal style; from that to the present day the instrumental style has been predominant. The masters of the former period wrote almost exclusively for the voice, and used the instruments only for the purpose of accompaniment. Even where Mozart and Haydn write so-called absolute * music, they always remain under the

* The word absolute is used by Franz as almost synonymous with instrumental, and must not be taken in the sense as

influence of the older style, and only in rare cases venture out of this sphere. Since Beethoven this has become different. The enormous genius of this man, whose chief power lay in his sway over the instruments, could not allow the existing forms, to limit its inspiration. He therefore was eagerly intent upon remoulding these forms according to his own requirements. The great pliability of the instruments considerably assisted this purpose, and it is well known how, in the course of his colossal development of the tone-material, Beethoven was led to the ultimate limits of his power."

After a few more remarks on his view of the *formal* liberation of music through Beethoven (which view I must ask the reader to compare with what on a former occasion has been said about the *spiritual* or *poetical* liberation of our art by that great reformer) Franz proceeds to ask: "But what are the essential points of difference between the vocal and instrumental forms of musical expression? The natural limitation of the voice could not but create such forms as were in accordance with it. Moreover the mechanism of the human organ ne-

applied by me throughout, in which sense Mozart and Haydn did indeed write nothing but absolute music.

cessitated a sequence of intervals which presented no serious difficulties to being perceived by the ear and rendered by the voice. In this way the so-called "strict (*strenge*) style" was formed. Here every note must, for the mentioned reasons, be the necessary complement of both its predecessor and successor; the free choice of expression being entirely excluded, by the strict rules of the style. This same regularity moreover applied equally, not only to the melody but also to the accompanying parts, barring of course the characteristic modifications as required for *alto*, *tenore* and *basso*. The same style had, for the sake of conformity to extend even to the accompanying instruments.

But also in cases where these instruments were used quite independently (as for instance, in Bach's and Handel's compositions for the orchestra, the organ, and the pianoforte), the "strict style" never quite relinquished its character; everywhere we meet the same, or at least similar, phenomena of vocal adaptability. One could, for instance, change a number of fugues in the 'Wohltemperirte Clavier' into beautifully-sounding choruses, without any essential alterations in the parts. Of Handel, it is known that he transferred some of his fugues for the pianoforte into his oratorios, developing them at the same time into tremendous choruses.

Beethoven, as I said before, reversed all this from top to bottom. The much greater velocity of the instruments and their infallible accuracy in rendering every sequence of notes, gradually supplanted the logical progress of the voices in the sense of the strict style. Henceforth, all the single parts moved with a freedom which, in Beethoven's last period, almost surpassed the limits of the possible.

The masters following immediately in Beethoven's footsteps, viz., Schubert, Chopin and Schumann (I except Mendelssohn, who takes an intermediate position between the two styles), carried on the thus created instrumental style, and transferred it as a rule even to specifically vocal pieces, reversing, in this way, exactly the habit of former centuries; hence the sometimes justified complaints about the want of adaptability to the voice in the works of modern masters.

On the other hand, it is utterly comical to hear modern critics deplore the way in which Bach and Handel treated the human voice like an instrument. But then, the world is turned topsy turvy."*

Franz goes on to relate, how the conditions of the true vocal style, to which the spirit of modern music is thoroughly adverse, were preserved in his artistic consciousness by means of the early studies and impressions alluded to in our biographical sketch, and how in consequence the same "strict style" prevailed to a certain extent in the accompaniments of his songs, which otherwise are so thoroughly imbued with the unfettered flow of subjective passion. It is, indeed, this vocality (if I may coin the word for my purpose), of the pianofore parts which, as I said before, gives their peculiar character to the songs of Franz, and sometimes leads to effects of great poetic beauty and originality.

4

Notwithstanding the importance of the question

* I must remind the reader that Franz is speaking of the voice in a purely musical sense. On the other hand, it is but too true that these masters, like most or all of their contemporaries, neglected the *poetical* side of the human voice as the enunciator of the words, and in this sense often did treat it like any other instrument.

at stake, and the more than ordinary ability with which it has been treated by Franz, I must almost fear that the reader will think this sojourn, in what he might call the outer court of the temple of song, of rather too long duration. But the accompaniment of the modern song forms so essential a part of its structure, that, to remain in the simile, it might almost be described as its foundation and corner stone; and, moreover, the quoted remarks bear to a great extent also on the melodious formation of Franz's songs. For we are often struck in his motives by a touch of sweet quaintness, which seems to transport us imperceptibly into the times of the great cantor of the Leipsic 'Thomasschule,' or, still further back, to the assemblies of the earliest Lutheran congregations, whose chants the stout, though tender hearted, reformer, compared to angelic harmonies. From thence to the pristine simplicity of the original Volkslied there is but one step, and we are not surprised to find our composer at his best in the artistic reproduction of popular *naïveté*. Such songs as 'Zur Strassburg auf der Schanz,' or 'Ich weiss ja warum ich so traurig bin,' the words of which are taken from the poesy of the people, display in the simplicity of their modulations, an affinity with the most primitive forms of human feeling, attainable only in that state of second childlike unconsciousness which is the truest sign of high artistic faculty.

The songs with words by Burns, which form a not inconsiderable part of Franz's compositions, belong to the same class of popular types. Here, however, we miss sadly that peculiar kind of weirdness, which forms the charm of the old national tunes to which Burns adapted his poems. Franz has rendered, and rendered admirably, what is purely lyrical in the Scottish poet, without, as far as I can see, even attempting to imitate the national colouring, which, it is true, has to a great extent disappeared in the German translation. The same applies, and very likely for the same reason, to Schumann, and many other German composers who were naturally attracted by the intense singing quality in Burn's works, so rarely met with in British poets. This want of perception is all the more remarkable amongst a nation which, as a rule, is of such easy access to foreign peculiarities, and which, moreover, prides itself particularly on its unbounded admiration for the great lyrist. The only German composer who seems, by some process of intuition, to have caught the musical spirit of our northern fellow islanders, is Beethoven, in whose accompaniments to Scotch tunes one is occasionally struck by a touch of the drawling sadness or rhythmical wildness of the genuine bagpipe. What this affinity consists in, or where its origin may be found, I am unable to say, seeing that Beethoven never set foot on British soil. I am only speaking from an undefined impression of my own experience.

As another point of resemblance with the spirit of the Volkslied, we mention in Franz, his predilection for the strophic treatment of his songs. They are generally founded on a melody of great simplicity, to which he adheres sometimes even where the altered character of a stanza seems to require the stronger contrast of a new motive. But if, in such cases we occasionally deplore the concession made by the poet to the musician, we cannot, on the other hand, refuse our highest admiration to the manner in which Franz, by a slight alteration in melody or accompaniment, produces the most striking effect of at once musical and poetical beauty. In one of his finest songs, called *Herbstsorge* (autumn sadness), by Osterwald, the sudden hope of a new spring is rendered with astonishing brightness by a slight change of the motive and the introduction of A natural instead of A flat, into the accompanying chord. The same applies to another song of equal beauty, but of a very different character from the subdued sadness of the mentioned autumnal elegy. I am speaking of our composer's setting of Heine's dreadful words 'Ja, du bist elend und ich grolle nicht,' in which the sullen despair of disappointed love is rendered by the continuous, one might almost say obstinate, recurrence of one short melodious phrase. The effect is one of surprising realism, and almost more forcible than the unsuppressed cries of despair which have made the setting of the companion poem 'Ich grolle nicht' by Schumann, so famous. But here, again, we are surprised in Franz's composition, at the wonderful subtleness of feeling with which a short *cantabile* phrase is made expressive of the momentary abatement of angry passion, as the lover mentions the hidden tears of her, whose falseness is the cause of his misery. The last mentioned song we also recommend to the consideration of those of our master's admirers who have invested him with a kind of pacifying, or, as they call it, "ethic" tendency, in contrast to the melancholy hopelessness of Schubert, and the undisguised Byronism of Schumann. I must confess that I have looked in vain for this feature. Such works as the setting of the utterly desperate words by Heine, 'Verfehltes Leben, verfehlte Liebe,' show but too well, how deeply Franz is imbued with the pessimistic spirit of our latter days, although, perhaps, he does not always utter it with the intensity of the two first mentioned composers. It is indeed, this common atmosphere of modern thought and passion which links these three men together, and has given rise to the hackneyed notion of their triumvirate on the Parnassus of German song. Such an arbitary combination is, indeed, quite as uncalled for as the careful measuring by the yard of their comparative merits. It is undeniable that all of them have certain peculiarities of their own, as Schubert his melody and dramatic force, Schumann his intensity of pointed effects, or Franz his subtelty of psychological detail in which they are superior to the others; but to extol these merits of the one with a view to disparaging his rivals, is a sign of partisanship of the blackest dye. The only answer to such barren haggling is the slightly modified phrase of Goethe, "that people ought to be glad to have three such big fellows:" perhaps we shall even have to add a fourth one to the number.

The independence of our composer's genius, is shown indirectly by the fact that, wherever he does imitate unconsciously (as his situation of a beginner with the admired examples of perfectly developed masters before him, made it almost impossible to avoid), he at once gives signs of flagging inspiration and literally ceases to be himself. This applies especially to such cases where Franz chooses words which have previously been set by other masters, without being able to justify this pleonasm by a new musical light thrown on the subject. His setting, for instance, of Heine's "Leise zieht durch mein Gemüth," is conceived in exactly the same spirit as the charming music to the same words by Mendelssohn, and, therefore seems to lack every *raison d'être*. In such cases priority ought to decide, or, at least, the perfect translation of a poem into the musical language ought to prevent a second attempt in the same direction, *unless*, as we said before, this second attempt starts from an essentially different basis.

Another danger by which the finest intentions of Franz have, in a few cases, been frustrated, is connected with the choice of his words. Sometimes this happens through a want of *rapport* between poet and composer; the extreme conciseness and drastic pointedness of some of Heine's shorter poems, for instance, seems occasionally to have prevented the beautiful broadness of Franz's *melos* from showing to its greatest advantage. In such cases we miss the more forcible, but (to use a common expression,) also more short-winded impressivenesss of Schumann's utterance.

At other times Franz has composed words in which the want of real feeling is only imperfectly hidden by an acquired smoothness of diction. In consequence the inspiration of the composer begins at once to flag, like the sails of a vessel when the breath of heaven ceases to blow. It is, indeed, always with some apprehension that we see the name of a minor poet on the title page of one of Franz's songs, excepting only that of W. Osterwald, whose tenderness and truth of feeling make up fully for what he wants in originality of thought and expression.

But, as I said before, it is just in this sympathetic dependence on the assistance of the words, that the poetical nature of our composer's talent is shown; we may call this, indeed, one of those amiable weaknesses which make us only the more prone to love and admire the truly great and admirable qualities of his muse.

Nowhere does this muse appear more loveable than where she is matched in the bonds of poetry with the noble and elevated, though melancholy, genius of Nicolaus Lenau. The rich gifts and tragic fate of this great poet would alone fill a volume. Be it said here that amongst German lyrists he takes his place immediately after Heine, to whom he is inferior in range of subject and *verve* of utterance, but whom he surpasses in purity of feeling. It is in his setting of Lenau's *Schilflieder* that we must recognise the most sustained effort of Franz, and we can, indeed, not find a better description of his muse—as she looks at us out of her large and quiet, but inexpressibly sad eyes,—than in the following lines of Lenau, which, clad in the beauty of Franz's melody, may be considered as at once the symbol and the triumph of his art :

Rest on me thou eye of darkness,
Wield thy undivided might;
Mildly earnest, tender, dreamy,
Fathomlessly darkest night.

With thy dark, thy magic shadow,
Hide away this world from me,
Only thou, above my being,
Biding everlastingly.

5.

There is no greater contrast imaginable than that between the quiet changeless life of Robert Franz in a small German town, and the brilliant career of Franz Liszt, the spoiled favourite of Europe, to which we have now to give a passing glance. After the many disappointments and miseries, through which we had to go with the men of genius who form the subjects of the preceding chapters, we feel almost relieved in turning, at the end of our journey, towards the sunniest regions of fortune and success. If ever the gods can be said to have showered their richest gifts without reserve or drawback on the cradle of a single mortal, this cradle must have been that in which Franz Liszt was, let us hope, duly deposited at Raiding, a small Hungarian village, on the day of his birth, the 22nd October, 1811.

From his first appearance in public, the fiftieth anniversary of which has been just celebrated at Pesth, his genius was acknowledged with an enthusiasm in which the whole musical republic, from Beethoven down to the obscurest dilettante, joined unanimously. The history of music knows of no success approaching the unprecedented and still unequalled applause with which the phenomenal achievements of the young pianoforte hero were received by enthusiastic audiences from Madrid to St. Petersburg. And the same success accompanied him in everything he undertook in life. When tired of the shallow fame of the virtuoso, he exchanged the honours of the pianist for the thorny career of the composer, he had, it is true, at first to suffer from the obstacles with which popular indifference and professional ill-will tried to impede his progress; but these impediments were soon overcome by his dauntless energy, and Liszt is at the present time living to see his works expanding daily in the public admiration of his contemporaries. Also as a conductor he added fresh laurels to his wreath.

But, better than all this, nature has endowed him with a true and genial heart, full to overflowing with sympathy for the joys and sufferings of others, and alien to any feeling of selfishness and envy. So we need not wonder at seeing that, to crown his happiness, the friendship of man and the love of woman were never absent from his course of life.

It would be impossible to condense an ever so short account of a career, so rich in important and interesting events, into the frame of a single chapter; we will fix only upon one circumstance, as at once important for the history of music and illustrative of the noble generosity of Liszt's nature, his friendship with Wagner. In thinking of the many temptations to mutual animosities and misunderstandings, to which the minds of two men living in the brightest light of public fame are exposed, one is struck with agreeable wonder at the ungrudging love and admiration between Wagner and Liszt, which finds its prototype and equal only in Schiller's and Goethe's friendship. The thought of rivalry seems never to have entered their minds, although the zeal of enthusiastic partisans can never have been absent, to fan the slightest spark of an ungracious feeling into a flame. But for more than twenty years both Liszt and Wagner have worked for the same purpose of artistic reform in their individual spheres, and not once has the source of purest friendship been tainted by a drop of bitterness. For an account of the origin and circumstances of this friendship we borrow the eloquent words of Wagner himself.

The following sketch, written in 1851, takes us back to the time when, after the revolution of 1849, Wagner, as the reader will recollect, had to fly the country, and in this way was cut off from all artistic *rapport* with his friends at home. "Again"—Wagner says—" I was thoroughly disheartened from undertaking any new artistic scheme. Only recently I had had proofs of the impossibility of making my art intelligible to the public, and all this disgusted me with the beginning of new dramatic works. Indeed, I thought that everything was at an end with my artistic creativeness. From this state of mental dejection I was raised by a *friend*. By most evident and undeniable proofs he made me feel that I was not deserted, but, on the contrary, understood deeply by those even who were otherwise most distant from me; in this way he gave me back my full artistic consciousness.

"This wonderful friend has been to me *Franz Liszt*. I must enter a little more deeply upon the character of this friendship, which to many has seemed paradoxical. Indeed, I have been compelled to appear repellent and hostile on so many sides, that I almost feel a want of communication about this our sympathetic union.

"I met Liszt for the first time during my earliest stay in Paris, and at a period when I had renounced the hope, nay, even the wish, of a Paris reputation, and, indeed, was in a state of internal revolt against the artistic life I found there. At our meeting Liszt appeared to me as the most perfect contrast of my own being and situation. In this world, into which it had been my desire to fly from my narrow circumstances, Liszt had grown up, from his earliest age, so as to be the object of general love and admiration, at a time when I was repulsed by general coldness and want of sympathy. . . . . In consequence I looked upon him with suspicion. I had no opportunity of disclosing my being and working to him, and, therefore, the reception I met with on his part was altogether of a superficial kind, as was indeed quite natural in a man to whom every day the most divergent impressions claimed access.

But I was not in a mood to look with unprejudiced eyes for the natural cause of his behaviour, which, friendly and obliging in itself, could not but hurt me in that state of my mind. I never repeated my first call on Liszt, and without knowing or even wishing to know him I was prone to look upon him as strange and adverse to my nature.

"My repeated expression of this feeling was afterwards told to Liszt, just at the time when my *Rienzi* at Dresden attracted general attention. He was surprised to find himself misunderstood with such violence by a man whom he had scarcely known, and whose acquaintance now seemed not without value to him. I am still touched at recollecting the repeated and eager attempts he made to change my opinion about him, even before he knew any of my works. He acted not from any artistic sympathy, but led by the purely human wish of discontinuing a casual disharmony between himself and another being; perhaps he also felt an infinitely tender misgiving of having really hurt me unconsciously. He who knows the regardless selfishness and dreadful insensibility in our social life, and especially in the relations of modern artists to each other, cannot but be struck with wonder, nay, delight, by the treatment I experienced from this extraordinary man. . . . Liszt soon afterwards witnessed a performance of *Rienzi* at Dresden, on which he had almost to insist: and after that I heard from all the different corners of the world, where he had been on his artistic excursions, how he had everywhere expressed his delight with my music, and, indeed, had — I would rather believe — unintentionally canvassed people's opinions in my favour. This happened at a time when it became more and more evident that my dramatic works would have no outward success. But just when the case seemed desperate, Liszt succeeded by his own energy in opening a hopeful refuge to my art.

"He ceased his wanderings, settled down at the small, modest Weimar, and took up the conductor's baton, after having been at home so long in the splendour of the greatest cities of Europe. At Weimar I saw him for the last time, when I rested a few days in Thuringia, not yet certain whether the threatening prosecution would compel me to continue my flight from Germany. The very day when my personal danger became a certainty, I saw Liszt conducting a rehearsal of my *Tannhäuser*,

T

and was astonished at recognising my second self in his achievement. What I had felt in inventing this music, he felt in performing it: what I wanted to express in writing it down, he said in making it sound. Strange to say, through the love of this rarest friend I gained, at the moment of becoming homeless, a real home for my art, which I had longed for and sought for always in the wrong place. . . . .

"At the end of my last stay at Paris, when ill, miserable, and despairing, I sat brooding over my fate, my eye fell on the score of my *Lohengrin*, totally forgotten by me. Suddenly I felt something like compassion, that this music should never sound from off the death-pale paper. Two words I wrote to Liszt; his answer was, the news that preparations for the performance were being made on the largest scale that the limited means of Weimar would permit. Everything that men and circumstances could do, was done, in order to make the work understood. . . . . Errors and misconceptions impeded the desired success. What was to be done to supply what was wanted, so as to further the true understanding on all sides, and with it the ultimate success of the work? Liszt saw it at once, and *did* it. He gave to the public his own impression of the work in a manner, the convincing eloquence and overpowering efficacy of which remain unequalled. Success was his reward, and with this success he now approaches me, saying: 'Behold we have come so far, now create us a new work, that we may go still further.'"

Besides *Lohengrin* and *Tannhäuser*, also the *Flying Dutchman* was successfully performed under Liszt's direction. But his noble zeal was not limited to the reproduction of the works of one man, however great that man might be. When, in 1848, Liszt closed his career as a virtuoso, and accepted a permanent engagement as conductor of the Court Theatre at Weimar, he did so with the distinct purpose of becoming the advocate of the rising musical generation, by the performance of such works as were written regardless of immediate success, and, therefore, without him would have stood little chance of ever seeing the light of the stage. In short intervals eleven operas of living composers were either performed for the first time or revived on the Weimar stage. Amongst these we count such works as *Benvenuto Cellini* by Berlioz, Schumann's *Genevieve*, and the same master's music to Byron's 'Manfred.' Schubert's *Alfonso and Estrella* was also rescued from oblivion by Liszt's exertions.

For a time it seemed as if the small city in Thuringia was once more going to be the artistic centre of Germany, as it had been in the days of Goethe, Schiller, and Herder. From all sides musicians and amateurs flocked to Weimar, to witness the astonishing feats to which a small but excellent community of singers and instrumentalists were inspired by the genius of their leader. In this way was formed the nucleus of a group of young musicians, full of talent and enthusiasm, and inspired by the noble example of Liszt, to spread a new evangel of supreme devotion to music and its poetical aims all over the world. It was, indeed, in those gatherings at Weimar that the musicians who now form the so-called School of the Future, till then unknown to each other and divided locally and mentally, came first to a clear understanding of their powers and aspirations. It need not be added how much the personal fascination of Liszt contributed to this desired effect. Amongst the numerous pupils on the pianoforte to whom he at the same period opened the invaluable treasure of his technical experience, we only mention Hans von Bülow, the worthy disciple of such a master.

6.

But, in a still higher sense, the soil of Weimar, with its great traditions, was to prove a field of richest harvest. When, in 1842, Liszt undertook the direction of a certain number of concerts every year at Weimar, his friend Duverger wrote the prophetic words, " Cette place qui oblige Liszt à séjourner trois mois de l'année à Weimar, doit marquer peut-être pour lui la transition de sa carrière de virtuose à celle de compositeur." The truth of this presage has since been proved by a long, brilliant list of compositions in different spheres of musical art, too long, indeed, and too brilliant to allow of an adequate survey of their number and merits within the limits of our present task.

Amongst the purest fruits of his creative labour we count his songs, to which we now will dedicate the few closing remarks of this work.

In Robert Franz we observed, combined with the desire of a poetically free expression, a strong reverential feeling for the abstract sacredness of the musical form, as shown in the strophic treatment of his songs. Liszt, on the contrary, has entirely freed himself from this awe; he is a poet, and nothing but a poet. His music, heard without the interpretation of the words, would in most cases seem an incoherent sequence of beautiful melodious snatches, interrupted by declamatory passages, and only connected by an indefinable continuance of sentiment which occasionally takes the form of what I have on a former occasion described as the "leading motive." The laws of tonality are continually violated by the abrupt introduction of the most divergent keys, and occasionally the metrical structure of the poem itself is obscured by the composer's dramatic vivacity. Here we have reached at last the consistent carrying out of the poetic principle in lyrical music to its final consequences.

The old dilemma between music and poetry and their mutual rights and duties rises once more before our eyes, but in a form which does not allow of the unconditional solution which we saw achieved in Wagner's music-drama. In the opera the forms of absolute music were a distinct encroachment on the domain of poetry, themselves founded on an unnatural basis, and therefore doomed to destruction from the beginning. But this is widely different in the Song. Here absolute music is represented by the *tune*, which, as we see in the Volkslied, is inspired only by the first stanza and afterwards repeated, regardless of changes in the sentiment of the words sung to it. The strict adherence to this principle in the artistic song is impossible, except in cases where either an imitation of the popular song is intended, or where the change in the emotional import of each single stanza is so slight as to make the same tune appear the most appropriate mode of expression for all of them. In all other cases this first melody must be abandoned and changed for another melodious or declamatory motive, according to the more or less lyrical or dramatic character of the words.

Still it cannot be denied that the absolute tune is closely connected with the original structure of the song, and that in abandoning it entirely for the freer expression of changing passion, the composer runs the risk of losing that principle of unity and consistent development of the musical part, without which the enjoyment of every work of art becomes impossible. It is true that this feeling of unity can to a great extent be supplied by the accompaniment, but it remains equally true that a great danger for the growth of modern song consists in the too independent treatment of the vocal part in the single stanzas, by which not only the musical beauty but also the rhythmical organism of the poem may be seriously injured. Even Wagner seems to acknowledge the existence of such a danger, and has in consequence treated the Song (wherever he introduces it into his dramatic works) much more on the absolutely musical principle than might be expected from him.

Franz Liszt's place is, to borrow a term from political life, on the extreme left, his principle being unlimited freedom with regard to both the melodious and rhythmical structure of his songs. It is true that some of his greatest effects he has achieved by purely melodious means, as, for instance, in that beautiful song "Es muss ein Wunderbares sein," which does not essentially differ from what we have described as the "through-composed" song, or in his setting of "Du bist wie eine Blume," where the recurrence of the first motive in the concluding bars of the vocal part is of sweetest suggestiveness. At other times a greater liberty in the rhythmical phrasing of the music is warranted by the metre of the poem itself, as, for instance, in Goethe's wonderful nightsong "Über allen Gipseln ist Ruh'" the heavenly calm of which Liszt has rendered by his wonderful harmonies in a manner which alone would secure him a place amongst the great masters of German song. Particularly, the modulation from G major back into the original E major at the close of the piece is of surprising beauty.

At other times however it cannot be denied that the extreme freedom of Liszt's rhythmical treatment has seriously injured the effect of his songs. The character, for instance, of Heine's popular words, "Ich weiss nicht was soll es bedeuten" is of too simple a kind to allow of the elaborate painting of details, and the introduction of new motives, as we find it in Liszt's otherwise beautiful and expressive music. I confess that the simple tune by Silcher, to which the Germans are used to chant these melancholy words (it is alleged at moments when they feel particularly jolly), seems to me more appropriate under the circumstances than our composer's ambitious effort. If I might venture a bold guess, I would say that this song, as well as the setting of Goethe's "King in Thule," were written at a time when Liszt was not yet quite free from the influence of the French *salon*, of the atmosphere of which, with its fashionable *Romance* they both remind one occasionally. The music to the last mentioned poem, I would further guess, must have been written originally for a French translation, for in the German version the declamation is faulty throughout.*

The same influence is traceable, but here with most beneficial effects, in Listz's compositions of some of Victor Hugo's songs. Particularly the charming setting of " Comment disaient-ils " displays the elegant grace of French spirit in its most favourable light, and is indeed a jewel of its kind.

In order to make the characteristic features of Listz's style quite plain, I think it will be best to compare one of his songs with the setting of the same words by another composer, which parallel will at the same time serve to show the variety of musical interpretations to which a single poem may give rise, according to the individualities of different masters. I have for this purpose chosen Heine's charming song. " Im Rhein " etc., which has been

* The reader must also remember that Liszt is Hungarian by birth and French by education, and that German is to him an acquired language.

set by both Robert Franz and Liszt, in a manner which in itself may be called absolutely beautiful, and the comparative value of which in each case it is far from my purpose to discuss.

I first subjoin an exact prose translation of the words, so as not to lose the slightest turn of sentiment or expression by an attempt at a metrical rendering.

> In the Rhine, the beautiful stream,
> There is mirrored in the waves,
> With its great cathedral,
> The great holy Cologne.
>
> In the cathedral there is a picture,
> Painted on golden leather;
> Into the wilderness of my heart,
> It has thrown its friendly rays.
>
> There are playing many roses and angels,
> Round our fair lady;
> The eyes, the lips, the cheeks,
> Resemble those of my love.

The emotional basis of this little lyric is a feeling of quiet, almost dreamy religiousness, as it may beseem a lover who, walking in the lofty aisles of a cathedral, sees the image of his beloved in the sweet countenance of every angel. This keynote

Franz has rendered most admirably in the simple notes of a beautiful melody, and the same feeling he sustains essentially unchanged from first to last. It is true that he emphasises the grandeur of the cathedral by a mezzoforte, and that on our entrance into the holy precinct we hear in the accompaniment something like the solemn chords of an organ, but upon the whole the flow of the melody remains uninterrupted by attempts at rendering single points of dramatic import. When at last the lover sees the resemblance between the virgin and his own heart's idol, his voice sinks into a whispered pianissimo, almost as if, struck with his discovery, he hesitated in giving utterance to his worldly longing. The whole piece bears the character of a sweet old legend, without a vestige of modern restlessness and passion.

Liszt opens his song with an introduction of four bars. A melodious phrase, rising and falling alternately suggests the festive ringing of a peal of bells, while the incessant roll of accompanying triplets renders with striking truth the splashing waves of a wide river. The vista of the great city by the majestic Rhine rises before our eyes, even before the voice begins to pronounce the first lines of the poem, always accompanied by the same expressive motive. At first the vocal part bears the quiet character of a narrative, till, at the mentioning of the holy city, the grandeur of the impression is illustrated by a *forte* passage of great dramatic effectiveness. The second stanza is a strict repetition of the first, both in harmony and melody, till the word "wilderness", which causes a change of modulation into minor keys till the words "friendly rays", at which the harmony suddenly emerges into a strain of brightest joy. At this point the pictorial motive in the accompaniment ceases, because of the heightened emotion, in which the impressions of the senses are no more noticed. It is in such touches of finest psychological observation, that Liszt's mastership appears in its most brilliant light.

The two following lines have given rise to a short effusion of intense religious beauty. The broken chords of the accompaniment seem to play round the voice, like the roses and angels in the wonderful old picture of the Cologne cathedral, of which the words speak. The last two lines are treated quite in the declamatory style, passing quickly by the ear like an enchanting, but, alas, too fugitive vision of delight. They are, however, repeated in broken utterances, as if the mind once more tried to recall the sweet message from the other world. But at the same time the sounds of the bells and of the rushing river are again heard in the accompaniment, and these carry us back into the sphere of the tangible world, till at last, with the softer and softer pianissimo of the chords, the whole scene wanes into rosy distance, like the glow of the setting sun.

Such is the character of Liszt's musical conception. We have pointed out before, the danger to which the beautiful flow of the melody is subjected by the frequent intrusion of purely poetical effects. But, on the other hand, the perfect blending of the two arts strikes the hearer with a feeling of beauty and harmony of a higher order, because it arises from the mutual surrender of two divergent elements in one common effort. In works like this, Liszt has brought the efficiency of music for poetical purposes to a pitch formerly unknown in lyrical compositions; in adding, moreover, that this music is, absolutely speaking, of great intrinsic beauty, I think I have said sufficient to show, that in the hands of a master artistic song is capable of vying successfully with the other forms of musical art in their most advanced stages of progress.

APPENDIX.

APPENDIX I.

THE following is an account of the festival at Bayreuth on the occasion of the foundation-stone of the Wagner Theatre being laid. It has been thought worth inserting here, as bearing in general upon the subject of this book, and still more, as exhibiting the vivid impression which the wonderful conducting of Wagner made on all those present.

Bayreuth, May 22nd, 1872.

IT is now scarcely ten years ago since Wagner, in the preface to his dramatic version of the *Nibelungen Saga*, first hinted at the possibility of having his great work performed by the voluntary assistance of the friends of his art. The chances of such an enterprise were at that time the most unfavourable that could be imagined. Although the success of Wagner's first four operas, wherever they had been adequately performed, was an undeniable fact, still his more advanced ideas of the fundamental reorganisation of the music-drama had found so little responsive sympathy amongst the German nation—if such a

U

nation could be said to exist at all—that the utter derision with which his appeal was received by the hostile press seemed but too well justified.

Amongst the causes which have removed all these obstacles and have now assembled a crowd of enthusiastic admirers at Bayreuth, I would mention —besides the irresistible power of his genius as realised in the successive works of Wagner—the great political events of the last two years, in which the various German tribes, so long divided by internal animosities and party struggles, have at last recovered the feeling of solidarity. For a philosophic people like the Germans, there soon arose the necessity for symbolising the newly recovered political unity in a work of artistic import; and it was therefore only natural to see the best amongst the nation turn towards the purest sources of old Teutonic inspiration, as Wagner has embodied them in his grand dramatic work. The master's call therefore for the means necessary to secure a worthy performance of his Nibelungen drama, was responded to with a most promising willingness; and it was the laying of the foundation-stone of a theatre to be erected for the purpose, that had assembled the friends of Wagner from all parts of the world.

I shall not intrude upon your space with a description of the ceremony, which proved a failure because of a most pertinacious rain, nor of the banquet, the horrors of which from a culinary point of view would be scarcely realisable to the English mind. The programme of the concert which formed the most interesting feature of the Bayreuth festival consisted only of the Ninth Symphony of Beethoven, preceded by Wagner's *Kaisermarsch*, the latter being chosen mainly as a representative embodiment of German national feeling.

With great tact Wagner had refrained from entering into competition with Beethoven's gigantic work, and had concentrated all the energy of his mind in the desire of doing justice to his great teacher's aspirations. At the same time the choice of Beethoven's Symphony in D Minor was the most appropriate that could be made on this occasion, because it forms as it were the foundation of the great development of modern German, and especially of Wagner's own, music. The principle of this new phase in art, as the present writer has expressed it on former occasions, is the necessity of a poetical basis of music; that is to say, a latent impulse of passionate inspiration which guides the composer's hand,

and the conditions of which are in themselves by far superior to the demands of music in its independent existence. The rules arising out of these demands are in the Ninth Symphony violated, nay, completely overthrown, with a freedom of purpose and grandeur of conception that can be explained only from Beethoven's fundamental idea, as it gradually rises to self-consciousness in the words of Schiller's ode 'An die Freude.'

In his celebrated programme to the Ninth Symphony, which Wagner wrote five-and-twenty years ago, he has interpreted Beethoven's poetical intentions by illustrative quotations from Goethe's 'Faust,' connecting in this way the two greatest works that German genius ever conceived. He there declares this symphony to be the struggle of the human heart for happiness. In the first movement this longing for joy is opposed and overshadowed by the black wings of despondency. In the plaintive notes of the orchestra we hear the sad burden of Faust's words:

"Entbehren sollst Du, sollst entbehren."

The second movement, on the other hand, with its quick and striking rhythmical formation, describes that wild mirth of despair which seeks respite and nepenthe in the waves of physical enjoyment. The trio again might be considered as a dramatic rendering of the village scene in 'Faust.' The adagio, with its sweet pure harmonies, appears after this like a dim recollection of former happiness and innocence—

"So sad, so strange the days that are no more."

In the fourth movement at last Beethoven leaves the limits of his own art entirely. The repetition of the main motives of the foregoing movements, always interrupted by the tremendous recitative of the double basses, is absolutely unexplainable from a purely musical point of view. It is the highest effort of dramatic characterisation, instrumental music has ever made, and seeing that it has reached the limits of its own proper power, it has to call the sister art of worded poetry to it said. Beethoven has done this in a way "in which," to speak with Wagner, "we do not know whether to admire more the master's bold inspiration or simple *naïveté*." To the grand choral piece which follows, the words of Schiller's ode form the best comment.

It is obvious how the introduction in this way of

words as the necessary complement of musical expression even at its climax of perfection became the stepping-stone to the further development of poetical music, as we discern it in what is generally called the "music of the future." It is equally clear that it requires more than the common intellect of the general run of conductors to grapple with the intellectual (not to speak of the musical) difficulties of such a work. Hence there is scarcely another composition in existence, which has been injured so much by the traditional routine of musical Philistinism. I candidly confess that, although I have heard the Ninth Symphony at least three score and ten times, I never quite understood its wonderfully grand and harmonious structure till to-day. Wagner indeed seems the born interpreter of this monumental work of musical genius. With a marvellous power of congenial receptivity, he conceives the grand intentions of his master Beethoven, and moreover he is in a most eminent degree a *conductor*.

It is difficult to say what are the mysterious conditions of musical leadership; they are certainly nearest akin to the qualities of a great military commander; and one can only agree with good old

Emperor William, who, himself entirely innocent of musical knowledge, said after Wagner's late performance of Beethoven's C Minor Symphony, at Berlin, in his homely way: "Now you see what a good general can do with his army."

It is indeed one of the most interesting sights, to see the immediate *rapport* established between Wagner and his orchestra as soon as he raises his baton. Each individual member, from the first violinist to the last drummer, is equally under the influence of a personal fascination, which seems to have much in common with the effects of animal magnetism. Every eye is turned towards the master; and it appears as if the musicians derived the notes they play not from the books on their desks, but from Wagner's glances and movements. I remember reading in Heine a description of Paganini's playing the violin, and how every one in the audience felt as if the virtuoso was looking at, and performing for him or her individually. A gun aimed in the direction of many different persons is said to produce a similar illusory effect; and several artists in Wagner's orchestra and chorus assured me that they felt the fascinating spell of the conductor's eye, looking at them during the whole performance. Wagner in common life is of a rather reserved and extremely gentlemanly deportment; but as soon as he faces his band a kind of demon seems to take possession of him. He storms, hisses, stamps his foot on the ground and performs the most wonderful gyratory movements with his arms; and woe to the wretch who wounds his keen ear with a false note. At other times, when the musical waves run smoothly, Wagner ceases almost entirely to beat the time, and a most winning smile is the doubly appreciated reward of his musicians, for a particularly well-executed passage. In brief, Wagner is as great a virtuoso on the orchestra as Liszt on the pianoforte, or Joachim on the violin, etc.

APPENDIX II.

LETTERS OF ROBERT SCHUMANN.

THE subjoined are a series of letters by Robert Schumann, written between 1835 and 1844, to Herr Anton von Zuccalmaglio, one of the most devoted contributors of the 'Neue Zeitschrift für Musik,' living at that time in the house of Prince Gortschakoff, at Warsaw. The MSS. are in my possession, and have been published in the 'Academy.' They afford valuable material for the great composer's life and literary career and will gain in interest if read in connection with the biographical facts related in the third chapter. For this reason it has been thought desirable to rescue them from the comparative obscurity in the columns of a journal. As to their literary merits, it must be confessed that, compared to the letters of Mendelssohn, they seem deficient in expression and void of those lively touches which have made the latter almost as popular as their author's compositions. But it ought to be borne in mind that Schumann's reserved nature was wont to discover its higher aims and deeper feelings rarely, and only to those nearest to him.

(1)

[*Dictated.*]

"*Leipzig,* 11*th August* 1835.

"Dear Sir,—It was not till some weeks ago that we received your MSS., and are delighted to find that our young institution [the 'Neue Zeitschrift'] has found an echo in the far North.

"The letter you contributed is a capital parody of certain epistles in German newspapers. Your Wedel,* the village sexton, is an excellent idea, and admirably adapted for our journal. Both the papers will shortly be printed. As to the printing of your poems, I hope you will have a little patience, as we have arrears which will take half a year to clear off.

"Won't it be possible for you to send your communications by a shorter route? With many

---

* One of Zuccalmaglio's pseudonyms.

thanks for your kind interest and hoping to receive other contributions,

"Yours faithfully

"The Editor,

"R. SCHUMANN."

Schumann adds a note in his own handwriting:—

"Your second letter of August 5th has this moment arrived. This goes by post in order to set your mind at rest about your excellent papers; the answer to your second will follow in the bookseller's parcel in a few days. One or the other will, I hope, reach you. In any case, favour us soon with something new. If you like our musical paper, you will greatly oblige me by mentioning it occasionally.

"R. SCHUMANN."

(2)

"Dear Sir,—First of all my best thanks for your new contribution. There is something in your articles which pleases me, but for which I cannot yet find the right name, unless it be the quiet way in which you dive down to the deepest places of the soul, and the clear exposition you give of what you have seen when you reappear on the surface. Continue to delight us by going on.

"Your capital proposal to supply a new text to Mozart's operas I quite agree with; but I have my doubts whether you will be able to carry it through. We know what publishers are, not to speak of managers, and especially the public, when they have once taken an idea into their heads; however, try it. As far as I am concerned, I am quite at your service, so long as I have nothing to do with the commercial side of the question, of which I am supremely ignorant. Have the kindness to let me know more of your plan, whether it includes any structural alteration in the plot, or only a text better adapted to the score, and so forth, in order that I may consult a publisher here about it.

"There is another thing which is rather on my mind. You know how difficult every undertaking is at the beginning. Our new journal meets with an unusual amount of sympathy; but yet I am working almost entirely without pay. If you are not compelled to live by your pen, clever, excellent as it is, I hope you won't mind waiting a little while longer for the usual *honoraire*. But if this is to be a bar to your sending us further contributions, consider the previous sentence cancelled. I accept all your conditions. On this point please send me your decision at once.

"Yours truly,
"R. SCHUMANN.
"*Leipzig*, 28/9, '35."

(3)

"*December* 17*th*, '35.

"Dear Sir,—Two things very different from one another have prevented my answering your letter before; I have been travelling, and I have been ill.

"First of all, about the publication of your manuscripts, a matter in which I take the warmest interest. I have knocked once and again at the publishers' doors for you. It is hard enough for principals to get any tolerable terms out of booksellers, let alone third parties. At last I found that the trees had prevented me from seeing the wood. My brothers are booksellers, and a firm, I think I may say, of good standing (Schumann brothers, at Zwickau), and they will be happy to take your metamorphosis of the text to Mozart, but only on condition that you share the loss as well as the profit. This, although I represented to them the inconvenience of such an arrangement. Now, you must decide, please. You can depend upon everything being above board, and upon their punctuality, whether you have a yearly or a shorter account with them. It will be better for you to apply direct to the house at Zwickau, in order to arrive at something definite.

"Your essays and letter I have. All excellent. Wedel has been declared member of the Davidsbund, whether you like it or not. Waldbrühl seems to me too obvious a pseudonym, so I have changed it to W. Brühl; you will forgive me. If you read our journal regularly (I hope you do, but should be glad to know for certain), you will stand some chance of improving your aquaintance with the Davidsbündler.

"We shall be glad of innumerable pages out of W.'s diary. If I can be of use in any other way, I am at your service. Do you know anything of the editor of the 'Volkslieder' (along with Baumstark, of Heidelberg)? Can you give me the names of some people *with a turn for poetry*, who could contribute to the journal?

"Yours very truly,
"R. SCHUMANN."

(4)

"*Leipzig, Good Friday*, 1836.

"Dear Sir,—I congratulate you heartily on your safe return. Don't keep me long waiting before you tell me about your adventures, and what you have seen; send an account of yourself as soon as you can. Something about Moscow would delight me especially. The name of Moscow always sounds in my ears like the sonorous stroke of a great bell. If you like the tone of the Davidsbündler letters from Augsburg, Berlin, Dresden, and Munich, you would do well to adopt it in your own. This is a good way of working up in an attractive manner a number of facts and circumstances; it gives a certain compactness and colour to the journal, and the people like it. You may picture to yourself the Davidsbund as a kind of spiritual brotherhood, though its visible branches are really pretty widely extended, and will in time, I hope, bear plenty of golden fruit. The secrecy of the thing possesses a great charm for many; and, like everything mysterious, a peculiar power. Not that your former letters from Warsaw did not please me exceedingly; indeed I regard them as some of the best in my journal, as I have told you several times. Your last letter but one enclosed the collection of the 'Mosellieder,' and two essays which by this time you will have read in print. The other MSS. ('Fest zu Malin' (?), etc. [name doubtful] are safe in the hands of my brother. Whether he will print the 'Mosellieder' even on commission, I have my doubts. He has at present a great undertaking on his hands, the *Universal Dictionary of Commerce*, by R. Schiebe, which employs a good deal of his time and resources. About the publication of your other manuscripts I hope soon to be able to tell you for certain, as I shall see my brother some weeks hence at the Leipzig fair. Your idea of laying the scene of a tale at Moscow, I think a particularly happy one. Perhaps I shall be able to do something for your manuscript, but can't promise yet. I long to receive your Moscow letters, and anything else from your pen. If you don't hear from me for a considerable time, you must put it down to a trip to the Rhine, whither I am thinking of going with Mendelssohn at the end of April.

I told Sonnenwald to send you your copy of the 'Zeitschrift' long ago, and have just stirred him up again to despatch it. You had better inquire at Sonnenwald's.

"Yours truly,

"R. SCHUMANN."

(5)

Leipzig, July 2nd, 1836.

"Dear Sir,—The reason for my long and ungrateful silence has lain in a good deal of distress of mind, out of which I found it impossible to rouse myself for work. It was music at last, and some original musical work of my own especially, and above all the restorative force of a young constitution, the woods and the green leaves, which have brought back courage and energy.* My first lines are to you. Like a child at a Christmas-tree, I stood before your presents, and turned them carefully over and over. Then I grow angry with myself that I can do nothing with the booksellers, and

---

* The crisis alluded to, exercised a highly favourable influence on his creative power, as we also see from a passage in a letter to his friend Dorn (dated 1839) in which Schumann, says "There is certainly much in my music of the struggle which it cost me to win Clara, and I am sure you have understood it."

can never get anything more encouraging than 'tomorrow' out of them, in spite of all my pains. And the worst of them all (though it must be said in his defence that he has a great deal of work on his hands) is my own brother, with whom, by the bye, your MSS. are all left. This is why I wanted to wait, so as to prepare a little surprise for you, but here I am again with empty hands. This of itself, after so much as I have received from you, is enough to make me sad. Have sent to G. Schwab; and shall to the 'Elegante Zeitung.' But why are you slow to write in your own name? I called on your friends as soon as I received the letter, which came to me by a round-about way. And when I took my chance of finding them at the Hôtel de Russie, they had just left. A great pity indeed. If you want a complete copy of the journal, please say so. Some weeks ago I sent you, through Sonnenwald, a parcel with all your essays, a pretty big collection. I read out your last letter but one to Mendelssohn: we both enjoyed it vastly. He says he doesn't care for male part-songs (*Männergesangquartette*), and doesn't think he can do anything in that way. I hardly think so either. But he will send you something next winter. Your oratorio I will forward him to Frankfort in a day or two, if he doesn't see it before in print. It seemed to make such an excellent beginning to my new volume that I anticipated your permission to publish it. The last four lines I should like perhaps a little altered: the repetition of 'fest' is a little disagreeable You will pardon my candour.

"My proposed journey to the Rhine (your native place, is it not?) never came about; my distress had quite knocked me down. Since that, however, some new airy shapes have found their way out of me: one of them I should like to bear your name, *i. e.* I should be glad to dedicate something to you.

"There are some things in my music which you will positively dislike, if I may judge from your former articles; but our new movement cannot fail to be intelligible, as a whole, to such a keen eye as yours, and is sure to meet with your sympathy and help. I seem to feel that we are standing at the beginning of a new time, and that strings may now be touched which have never been heard before. May the future be with it, and some good genius bring it to perfection.

"Good-bye for to-day. Send me whatever pearls you have in store. In my manifold occupations I want the assistance of others, and chiefly that of trustworthy men like yourself.

"Yours truly,
"Robert Schumann."

(6)

"*Leipzic, October* 18*th*, 1836.

"I received with joy everything you mention, and only wish it were more. A biographical sketch of [name illegible] would be particularly welcome to my readers and myself. To judge by one of your former letters, you seem to believe that some of your MSS. are not yet printed, but this is the case only with one—the dream about the prize symphony; sometimes I look at it with real reluctance. There is so much in it that I like, and yet I think it would do better for any other paper than the 'Neue Zeitschrift,' which once for all is devoted to youth and progress. Besides, the symphony of Berlioz has just been so favourably reviewed in our journal, that a new and entirely different opinion is more likely to puzzle the reader than to be of any use.

"Hr. Freier's songs are going to be noticed. On the publishers of this place I have no influence whatever. I think it better for Hr. Freier to apply direct to Hofmeister. I have tried myself several times to find a publisher for other people's MSS., but have met with so many refusals that I really don't care to ask any more. You can scarcely believe how sorry I am for being obliged to say this to you, to whom I owe so much.

"Will you be kind enough to go once more through your file of the 'Zeitschrift,' and tell me exactly what numbers are wanting. I sent you some time ago separate copies of all your articles; have you received them?

"A Warsawian composer, Nowakowski, who was here for some weeks, mentioned to me a musical periodical in the Polish language. Can you tell me at all what it is like? Last summer you announced to me a Moscowite friend of yours, but nobody has appeared yet. The musical season here is at its height. Lypinsky is sure to pass Warsaw. I like him very much, both personally and as an artist. I gave your MS. of the poem, 'Die Tonkunst,' to Mendelssohn; he sends his thanks and kind regards; but for the present he cares more for making love to his chosen than for composing.

"Have you seen the 'Papillons' and the sonata

by Florestan and Eusebius? I wish you would let me know your opinion of them at once. You will soon read a comprehensive article about them by Moscheles, who is now in London.* Don't you think it better to give sometimes another form to your contributions? Gottschalk † has become such a dear friend of mine that I should be sorry to miss him; but I am obliged to plead for my readers. Besides, new forms bring new ideas.

"Please ask me to do something for you which is very difficult, otherwise I shall be too light in the balance.

"I long for news of you; please send me your letters direct by post. New Year is coming on; do you know anything to begin the new volume with?

"Yours faithfully,
"ROBERT SCHUMANN."‡

* This sonata appeared under the title, 'Pianoforte-Sonate, Clara zugeeignet von Florestan und Eusebius,' Op. ii. Moscheles' criticism on it (dated London, October, 1836) may be found in Wasielewsky's 'Life of Schumann', 1st ed., p. 320.

† Gottschalk Wedel, the *nom de plume* of Zuccalmaglio, already explained.

‡ In order to explain the last letter, it is necessary to state the following facts. The Vienna Kunstverein had promised a prize to the composer of the best symphony. Herr

(7)

"*Leipzig, Jan.* 31, 1837.

"My dear Sir,—First of all I must tell you how I gave Mendelssohn, with whom I dine every day, your article, 'Erste Töne.' I stood aside and watched his face to see what impression would be made upon him by your last sentence, which I confess, had several times brought the tears into my own eyes. He read the article attentively; his face (what a glorious, divine face it is!) revealed all his impressions as he went on. The

von Zuccalmaglio seems to have been afraid the committee might decide in favour of Berlioz, or a composer of his school, and, to prevent this unpatriotic proceeding, he wrote, under his favourite pseudonym, 'Gottschalk Wedel,' the dream mentioned in the letter, which, notwithstanding its romantic form, showed a good deal of German Philistinism. In it he abuses Berlioz's dramatic symphony, 'Episode de la Vie d'un Artiste,' the great merits of which Schumann himself had gladly acknowledged in the article alluded to. Z.'s fear, however, proved to be unnecessary, for Lachner, a Munich composer, won the prize. Schumann inserted Z.'s article with a note of his own, in which he entirely disagrees with the views of his friend and of the Vienna committee. Schumann's and Z.'s article may be read now in the former's 'Gesammelte Schriften,' 2nd ed., i. 68. and 131.

further he got the more it seemed to light up, till at last he came to the passage: it was a pity you could not see him. 'Ha!' he cried, 'what's this? That is really too much; I am quite delighted. There are different kinds of praise, but this comes from a pure heart.' And he went on to say a great deal more. You should have seen him and heard him: 'Ten thousand thanks to the man who wrote this.' So we went on until we dived into our champagne.

"The fact is, as I have long ago made up my mind, 'there is no man who can write on music like Wedel;' and I think that I can read the same verdict in the delicate but continual motion of Mendelssohn's countenance, which is a record of all that is passing both within and without him. So full of life is each word of your prose, so picturesque are its little turns of expression, its cadences so melodiously falling and rising; but enough of this.

"Do you know his 'St. Paul,' in which one beauty relieves another without interruption? He was the first to grant to the Graces a place in the House of God, where they certainly ought not to be forgotten. Hitherto they have not been able to make their voices heard for the multitude of the fugues. Do read 'St. Paul,' the sooner the better. You will find in it nothing of Handel or Bach, whatever people may say, except so far as all church music must be alike.

"Many thanks for your manifestoes. The 'Erste Töne' I received with your letter of October 28th, only a fortnight ago.

"I wish I could see you and have a talk with you this summer, only I am sorry that you are not likely to find Mendelssohn here, as he hopes to spend the summer at Frankfort in the arms of his beloved. Since he has been engaged he has become quite a child.

"Have you got any *little poems for music* which might be published in my paper? For your tragedy I can't do anything. As soon as he heard the word 'tragedy,' Mr. Booth stared at me from top to toe, looking very much amazed. You had better collect your 'Wedeliana,' for which I shall hope to do something, with God's help.

"I am very anxious to hear your opinion on Florestan's sonata (the article about it in the 'Zeitschrift' was by Moscheles, as I think I told you before).

"Some one has just called, so farewell, and don't forget

"Your

"Schumann."

(8)

"*Leipzig, April* 16*th,* 1837.

"My dear Sir,—I had scarcely read your letter when my brother, the publisher of Zwickau, who had come for the Leipzig fair, entered my room, and in answer to my hasty question about the 'Mosellieder' told me they would be here in about seven days and in print. I was very much surprised to hear this, but am now rather afraid that it may have been done without your full consent. Please set me soon at ease about that. For the same reason I have retained the parcel for Menzel in Stuttgart, because you may now, perhaps, wish to dispose of it otherwise.

"The enterprising publisher, R. Freier of Leipzig, is engaged in printing your north-southern 'Furte.' Something occurs to me that might yet be done. Could you not add to these poems an introduction in prose, as Goethe has done so admirably to his 'Divan'? The number of unusual expressions ('Furte,' to begin with, was new to me) seems to require some explanation, which you might put in a poetical form.

"The 'Splitterrichter' I remember having read; but I must first search for it among my papers, which can't be done in a moment. If you are particularly in want of it, let me know.

"I shall be extremely glad to see you here. In me, however, you must not expect to find much. I scarcely ever talk, except in the evening, and most while playing the piano. The Florestan sonata, and the back numbers which are wanting, I prefer to give into your own hands. If you don't come soon, I am sorry to say, you won't find Mendelssohn nor Bennet* (an angel of a musician), but, in any case, David and Clara Wieck, both remarkable people.

"Write to me please as soon as possible, and send me heaps of articles; the world wants them. My paper has lately gained much ground. For the next volume I hope to come to an arrangement with another publisher, more favourable both to myself and my contributors. You are, of course,

---

* Sir William Sterndale.

the first I have to think of, and in whose debt I am deepest. Keep me in your kind remembrance.

"Yours truly,
"R. SCHUMANN."

(9)

Leipzig, May 18*th*, 1837.

"Be kind enough to receive at last from my hands the first copy of your 'Furte.' The Roman characters I do not like, but it was too late to change them. You will soon receive in a parcel several copies of the 'Furte' and also ten of your 'Mosellieder:' one of the latter, together with the tragedy, has been sent to Menzel in Stuttgart, so the most important things are settled.

"Of Bach's concerto in D minor only Mendelssohn has a copy. As soon as he comes back from the Rhine—that is, not before the end of September—I shall have it copied out for you and myself; I always considered it as one of the most admirable productions in existence.

"I am very sorry that you can't come, because I want to talk over several things with you which it would require a great deal of time to explain in writing. I have a variety of plans and schemes for which I want your assistance. First of all, I have thought for a long time of giving real life to the Davidsbund by bringing men of the same opinion (even if not professional musicians) in a closer connection by means of letters and symbols. If Academies, with dunces at their heads, designate their members, why should not we, the younger generation, nominate ourselves ? There is another idea which has a great attraction for me, and which, though of more general importance, might be connected with the former; that is, to found an *agency for publishing works of all composers* who would submit to its statutes. It would aim at preserving for the composer the profits which hitherto have been almost entirely absorbed by the publisher. The only thing required is to engage an agent for the business, whose rights would be legally secured. The composer would have to make a deposit for the publishing expenses of his work, and receive, say once a year, an account of the sale and the overplus due after the expenses have been paid. Thus much to-day. Please consider the matter carefully by yourself; perhaps it might be realised some day for the great benefit of composers. Please think about it and let me know your opinion.

I should have liked to sound you a little on another point, whether we might not publish together in a double work our past and future ideas on music, your 'Wedeliana' and my ' Davidsbündleriana.' For many of them it would be a pity that they should be buried in a periodical. My brother would be the publisher. All we should have to do would be to amalgamate our work in an interesting form, and on this point it would of course be necessary to come to some agreement.

"To all this, my excellent friend, I hope you will devote a few hours of your meditations. It seems to me often, as if I had not very long to live, and so I should like to do more work before I die. I am longing for your answer.

"Yours faithfully,
"ROBERT SCHUMANN."

(10)

Leipzig, August 20*th,* 1837.

" My dear Sir,—The reason why I have kept you waiting so long for an answer to so many kindnesses of yours, is partly because my hope for Mr. Ernemann's arrival is still a mere hope. I was anxious to tell him all I had to say, my esteem and all I feel for you. It now seems doubtful whether he will come at all; some weeks ago he sent from Dresden some manuscripts of yours; since then everything has been silent again.

"Now let us begin about our music. I am in some difficulty about your letter on Berlioz, as I was before about that of L., which really is exaggerated. May I tell you the reason why it was accepted? It is not a very noble one, but it is always best to speak out the plain truth. L. sent me the letter, and at the same time asked me urgently for money. This I gave him with pleasure; but then I did not wish to be the loser by it, and, besides, as I have worked for the paper for years, I don't want to pay money out of my own pocket; and so it happened. Besides—pardon me for saying so—you judge the overture without having *heard* it. *You have no idea* what he contrives to make out of the orchestra. If you have heard a *good* performance of the overture and still wish to have your article published, I shall do so with pleasure. Altogether the whole business is not worth all this trouble, and the point is more or less settled by a short notice of the overture in a former volume. My opinion as therein expressed seems to be quite correct even now. I am only sorry that you should have written your excellent article to no purpose. Perhaps you can propose a compromise.

"Your other letter I must keep back until things are more advanced. If I printed it now, and the foundation of my great German "Artistic Union" should afterwards come to nought, the effect would be rather ridiculous. So I must ask you to have a little patience.

"The article against Nikolai was remarkably good and carried conviction with it in every word. Don't forget to write more of that kind. By the bye, which concerto of Bach's do you want to have copied out—the one for three pianos, or that for one? Perhaps you would also like to have a copy of his great mass in B minor? I should like for once to make you one or two Christmas presents. Write and tell me what you wish to have.

"As for Freier's manuscripts, I sent them off to Messrs. Schott as early as the Easter fair. Haven't you received yet a copy of the 'Mosellieder?' They have been despatched safely from here, as well as the copies for your brother at Cologne. All the manuscripts you sent me are in my brother's hands.

He is so difficult to manage that I am sorry I have recommended him to you. Do you still like the idea of writing new words to Mozart's operas? To tell you the truth I think it impossible.

"I am over head and ears in work, and so must finish with my kindest regards and in the hope of an early answer.

"Yours truly,

" ROBERT SCHUMANN."

(11)

This letter refers almost entirely to private matters. I select the following characteristic passages:—

Leipzig, January 13*th*, 1838.

"I for my own part understand Berlioz as clearly as the blue sky above me. . . . . . I think there is really a new time in music coming. It must come. Fifty years have worked great changes and carried us on a good deal further."

And about Henselt—

"Ask him to play to you for hours together, and then only will you learn how to appreciate and admire him. Of all pianists (and I have heard all of them and often) he has given me the greatest pleasure."

(12)

Leipzig, August 8th, 1838.

"My dearest Friend,—I have to tell you an important piece of news to-day, but you must not let any one else hear about it. I should have preferred to communicate it to you personally, but now there is some uncertainty whether you will find me still here when you come in October. The thing is that the 'Zeitschrift' will appear from the 1st of January, 1839, at Vienna, where I am going myself at the end of September. I hope to derive much good by this change—a new round of life, new work, and new ideas. I think I can do a great deal where people swim in confusion 'like flies in the buttermilk,' as Jetter says. But now, my dear Wedel, give me your hand and promise me not to leave me in the lurch in my new place. I shall have many troubles to get over; and we shall have to go on rather gently, as the censorship is strict and will suppress freely.

"First of all, you would oblige me by sending

for some time to come as much MS. as you possibly can. From October till December my 'vocal' minister, Oswald Lorenz, is going to look after the editing of the journal, and I must not leave him in want of matter.

"In the second place, I want you to think about an article on the new arrangement, its consequences, etc., to grace the first number that appears in Vienna. You know how to manage this so delicately that I always like to let you have the first word, and I am sure to be prevented by business from undertaking work at any great length for the next time. Your introductory essay ought to be with me in Vienna by the end of November at the latest. My exact address I shall let you have before long.

"I am getting continually deeper and deeper in your debt, and I must ask you to think about settling accounts.

"Many thanks for all you have sent me lately; it is all going to be published by-and-by. Some of the musical quotations of Elsner's 'Passion Music' had to be left out, as they would have taken up too much room. But I thought whether the march, which is a whole in itself and which I also like extremely, might not be published in one of the next musical supplements. You would oblige by a line about that. Ernemann's songs smiled at me out of a heap of music, like blossoms, especially some of them; they will be noticed in the 'Zeitschrift.' Perhaps Ernemann has something (for four voices) in store for the supplements.

"Many thanks also for the 'Popular Songs,' although I must confess that I have not always been pleased with the accompaniment. At times it does not seem to be natural enough. But then of course I listen with the ears of a musician, and even in a popular song I can't stand fifths and octaves, although one sometimes meets with them in such pieces.

"Gottschalk will find his name on 'Kinderscenen,' which are going to appear under my own. He is sure to find some little pleasure in them, for they come from the bottom of my heart.

"A Nuremberg merchant brought me your letter and account. I gave him what I had—not much, I am sorry to say.

"Good-bye for to-day; I recommend my plans to your consideration, and hope to hear from you, or better to see you soon. "Yours,

"R. SCHUMANN."

(13)

Vienna, October 19*th*, 1838.

"My dear Friend,—I regret to hear that you have been in Leipzig without my being there to receive you, an event to which I have always looked forward with so much pleasure. But you are sure to have found a trusty companion in the excellent G [*name illegible*]. I am sorry you did not find *Idomeneo*, but you must not blame me for that. I had written to my brother immediately, but he was on his way to Leipzig, so the letter missed him, and this accounts for the delay. Have you not got it yet? I have reminded him again from here.

"Now, I should like to hear about yourself— how you are, and if you still remember me and the 'Zeitschrift.' I have not heard from Leipzig that you left anything for my paper. Have you forgotten all about the 'Baurede,' or have you anything else fit for the first numbers of the new volume, which is to come out in Vienna? The Viennese would like best something cheerful— story-like, not by any means Catilinarian, which they don't understand.

"At the same time, the publication of the 'Zeitschrift' in Vienna is not yet a settled affair. You can't believe how many difficulties the censorship makes, and also the publishers, who are frightened for the glory of their Strauss, Proch, and others. Still I hope to arrange it before the new year, and therefore ask you to send me your contributions for the next volume direct by post to *Vienna*. I long for a letter from you.

"Heuser the singer is here; he has a most complete collection of Bach's compositions, especially many unpublished pieces, and is glad to place at disposal what he is asked for. If you want anything that Mr. Ernemann does not possess, I'll have it copied out for you.

"About Vienna itself I have my own ideas; I don't think I am suited for these kind of people; their flippancy is really sometimes too much for me. Still a closer acquaintance with single individuals will, I am sure, modify my opinions in many respects.

"Keep me in kind remembrance. I now want my Wedel more than ever. Seyfried asked after you with the greatest interest.

"Now you know all I have to ask you; let me soon have a kind word from you.

"Yours truly,

"R. SCHUMANN."

(14)

Vienna, March 10th, 1839.

"My dear Sir and Friend,—Although I have not written to you for a long time, I have been constantly in intellectual intercourse with you. I always waited in order to tell you definitely about the settling down here both of myself and my paper. Now I am able to do so. Neither I nor my paper are to remain in this city, which I find is not the right place for either of them. After careful consideration, I came to the conclusion that the thing couldn't be done advantageously. The chief inpediment was the censorship. At the end of April, at the latest, I shall be back in Leipzig, with renewed strength to carry on my journal, which it must be confessed has suffered during my absence. Everything remains as it was; and I also hope to find your friendship unaltered. Your last letter, together with your Warsaw friend's contributions, I received some time ago; many thanks. The *Ave Maria* and *Jagdlied* by Ernemann I like very much, but of D'Alquen I am not able to say the same; he seems even wanting in technical skill. The essay 'Erste Töne' is exquisite. Next first of May I intend to constitute our 'Davidsbund' by means of an article in the 'Zeitschrift.' I should like you to read it first, were it not for the long distance which divides us. May I hope to find a letter from you in Leipzig? How are you, and what are you working at? The Stuttgart 'Nationalzeitung' is going to become a highly respectable bully, against which we must be on our guard. The editor is very weak as a musician, but he knows how to puff. But enough for this time, and don't forget

" Yours truly,

" SCHUMANN."

(15)

"*Leipzig, April 27th,* 1839.

" My dearest Sir and Friend,—I have returned safely, although the first thing I learned was the news of a death in our family. You will also understand that after the last half-year I had many arrears to get through; and that is why I have not answered your kind letter before now. The absence from my paper I believe has been to some advantage. It now smiles on me as young and fresh as when we first started it; and just now diligence and perseverance are more necessary than ever. The Stuttgart 'Universalist' begins to 'wax fat;' and notwithstanding his being an arch humbug, without, as I think, *the vaguest idea of music*, yet he knows how to manipulate words and titles, and therefore must be checked somehow. I can't understand how those old gentlemen, like Spohr, Schneider, and others, can let themselves be imposed upon by such a windy braggart. Perhaps he will make you also his corresponding member, as he did me without my knowledge. An impertinent fellow, with whom it is better to have nothing to do.

"I am glad to hear about the news which Mr. Ernemann has brought from Petersburg. I hope you'll think of me. Some time ago I received a note from Warsaw, signed Wahrlich, which complains of several things in your letters, etc. It did not seem important enough to send it on to you. I'll keep it for you in case you come to Leipzig. I hope you will come; I shall stay here in any case during summer. I hope that something of the [*word illegible*] will please you, especially if I play my own things on the piano, and am in a happy mood. I wish you would look at the 'Kinderscenen,' and say something about it with your genial Wedelian vein. My note-paper has come to an end. Only let me add my kindest regards.

"R. SCHUMANN."

(16)

"*Leipzig, Dec.* 31*st,* 1840.

"My dear Sir and Friend,—First of all I have to thank you for your ready assistance. You have recalled Thibaut's image to my mind in the most lively manner. Your paper adorns the first number of the new volume of the 'Zeitschrift,' for which I hope you will preserve your further kind sympathy.

"I am sorry I don't know R [*name illegible*] at all; but even if I did, it would be of no great use for your purposes. Every one describes him as an obstinate, stiff-necked fellow, who won't listen to advice. None of my friends are acquainted with him. The best thing for you is to send him your MS. to read. Have you no connections at Dresden—through Lüttichau, Miltitz, or Tieck? Your piece would be in the best hands there. Our comedy and tragedy are less than middling.

"I send you the 'Myrthen' and three little songs. Perhaps you will find an opportunity of having the songs sung to you by beautiful lips: they sound very nice; I heard them the day before yesterday. The 'Myrthen' of course give a deeper insight into the secret of my musical work. I wish I could have added my cycle of Heine's Songs; but I have no copy left. Several other things have also appeared lately about which I hope to converse with you before long. Music is sure to absorb me entirely; I always have to tear myself from it by force. But enough. Everything else I must tell you personally.

"I have still another question and favour to ask you. A certain Dr. v. Kaiserlingk of Berlin offers me his services as correspondent, on the introduction of the publisher. Do you know him at all? Hard experience has made me cautious. Perhaps you can tell me about him.

"I should wish to know your address; I don't like to get at you always through the medium of third persons. Also tell me when you are really coming to Leipzig.

"Please write to me soon, and keep me in kind remembrance.

"Yours truly,
"ROB. SCHUMANN.

"Hiller writes from Milan to say that he is engaged to the Polish lady we wot of. Did I tell you that he sent you a letter to Warsaw, addressed 'Gottschalk Wedel,' which you of course did not get?"

(17)

"*Leipzig, January* 23*rd*, 1844.

"My dearest Friend,—I have owed you an answer for a long time, and even now I can only send you a short note. I stand with one foot in the carriage to start for a long pilgrimage to Petersburg and Moscow. Before, I was prevented from writing by my indecision about the opera-text, and also by the performances of my *Peri* here and at Dresden. On both occasions I got much pleasure, and perhaps some honour. Now I should like to begin an opera soon; but for the present this northward journey compels me to abandon all plans and preparations of this kind. But how excellent it will be if I find some work to go on with on my return at the beginning of May. For this I hope you will give me your kind assistance. In spite of your objections, I have not yet abandoned *Mokanna*. But it is from the same book as the *Peri*, and the scene also Oriental; therefore I think I'll keep it for *a later period*. Best of all, I like your plan of the 'Invasion of Spain by the Moors.' Please think about it. I should be but too happy to find the drama finished for my return in May. This I wanted to ask you.

"Please don't forget the 'Zeitschrift' during my absence, and favour it with frequent contributions. I shall resign the editorship before long, but always take the greatest interest in its welfare.

"My kindest regards to you. Please address letter to the care of Friese as heretofore.

"Yours truly,

"ROBERT SCHUMANN."

THE END.

www.ingramcontent.com/pod-product-compliance
Lightning Source LLC
Chambersburg PA
CBHW031853220426
43663CB00006B/599